CLASSICAL LIBERALISM

Also by David Conway

A FAREWELL TO MARX: An Outline and Appraisal of his Theories

FREE-MARKET FEMINISM

Classical Liberalism

The Unvanquished Ideal

David Conway
Professor of Philosophy
School of Humanities and Cultural Studies
Middlesex University

Published in Great Britain by
MACMILLAN PRESS LTD
Houndmills, Basingstoke, Hampshire RG21 6XS
and London
Companies and representatives
throughout the world

A catalogue record for this book is available
from the British Library.

ISBN 0–333–64842–0 hardcover
ISBN 0–333–76052–2 paperback

Published in the United States of America by
ST. MARTIN'S PRESS, INC.,
Scholarly and Reference Division,
175 Fifth Avenue,
New York, N.Y. 10010

ISBN 0–312–12867–3 clothbound
ISBN 0–312–21932–6 paperback

Library of Congress has cataloged the hardcover edition as follows:
Conway, David.
Classical liberalism : the unvanquished ideal / David Conway.
p.   cm.
Includes bibliographical references and index.
ISBN 0–312–12867–3
1. Liberalism.   I. Title.
JC574.C66   1995
320.5'1—dc20   95–21527
                                                              CIP

First edition 1995
Reprinted 1998

This book is printed on paper suitable for recycling and made from fully managed and
sustained forest sources.

10   9   8   7   6   5   4   3   2   1
07   06   05   04   03   02   01   00   99   98

Printed and bound in Great Britain by
Antony Rowe Ltd, Chippenham, Wiltshire

To Caroline

Contents

Acknowledgements

This book was made possible through the award of a Bowling Green State University Visiting Scholar Fellowship. This award enabled me to stay at the Social Philosophy and Policy Center of Bowling Green State University, Ohio, during the Spring Semester of 1993, where the first draft was written.

I wish to register my special thanks to the Center's directors, Fred Miller, Jeffrey Paul and Ellen Paul, for making me feel so welcome and giving so generously of their time. I learned a great deal from each of them.

I should like also to thank Gerald Gaus and John Gray who were at the Center while I was there and from whom I benefited from discussion.

Thanks are also due to Alisdair MacIntyre and to his UK and US publishers, Duckworth and University of Notre Dame Press, for their kind permission to quote from the second edition of his book, *After Virtue*, London and Notre Dame, 1987.

Towards those on this side of the Atlantic, I owe a different amalgam of thanks. First, I must thank Middlesex University for having granted me leave to take up the Fellowship. Second, I owe thanks to Arthur Seldon for reading through and commenting upon an early draft. His many helpful suggestions have done much to improve the final version.

Finally, and above all, I am indebted to my wife, Caroline, for all she has done to make this book possible. It is to Caroline, fellow classical liberal and muse, that the book is dedicated.

DAVID CONWAY
Middlesex University

1 Introduction

The 1980s bore witness to two momentous political events. The first was a veritable renaissance of capitalism world-wide. The second was a no less dramatic decline in the fortunes of Soviet-style communism. The demise of communism culminated at the end of the decade in the collapse of the Soviet Union and the reunification of Germany. For one brief moment, the prospects for mankind never seemed rosier. Paeans were sung to the arrival of the end of history. It was confidently forecast that we could now all look forward to the enjoyment of perpetual peace and affluence safe within the citadels of liberal democracy.

Sadly, and all too soon, that brief euphoric moment has passed away. Today, the liberal democracies of the West find themselves once more plunged into the turbulent maelstrom of history. In the difficult and uncertain times of the present, to what political doctrine should nations of the West turn for guidance?

With the Soviet experiment having ended in such ignominious failure, it might have been expected that few in the West would harbour any lingering doubts as to the superiority to all alternatives of some form of liberal democratic capitalism. Indeed, for a period during the eighties, it seemed that, quite independently of the events unfolding on the other side of the Iron Curtain, Western societies had finally reached some kind of consensus on the overwhelming case for capitalism and for concomitantly limited government. As well as witnessing the decline and fall of Soviet-style communism, the 1980s also witnessed on both sides of the Atlantic the election to office of administrations that had been mandated – and seemingly were whole-heartedly determined – to roll back the frontiers of the state. It seemed as if the preceding decades of drift into ever-increasing state regulation and intervention were destined to be reversed.

Looking back with hindsight, it now seems clear just how limited and short-lived was the success of the Reagan and Thatcher governments in achieving their similar economic and social policy objectives. Neither was able to do much to reduce the proportion of gross national product expended by their respective governments. In both cases, the passing of these administrations has been followed by policy changes which have reversed the endeavour of these two former leaders to establish greater freedom for private enterprise and a more restricted role for government.

A variety of circumstances has conspired to bring about this reversal of trends. Shortly after the return to power of the Thatcher government in

1

1987, stock-market prices throughout the world experienced a dramatic 'crash'. The reverberations of this crash dealt to public confidence in the market a profound shock from which it was never fully to recover. This undermining of public confidence in the market was not least in part because the 'crash' was rapidly followed by a steep and protracted recession affecting all the leading economies.

Some observers have been quick to seize on both events as confirmation of the longheld conviction that capitalism is unable to operate except through very volatile and baneful economic cycles. No matter that the 'crash' was a mere temporary blip from which prices fully and quickly recovered as soon as the US Congress withdrew the threat to outlaw leveraged buy-outs the imposition of which had precipitated the collapse in prices in the first place. No matter also that the main cause of the recession was something equally entirely exogenous to capitalism. This was the cost of the reunification of Germany in 1990 which had two components. There was, first, the cost of unifying the German currency which was done in a way which allowed former East Germans to exchange their old currency for German marks at a rate which grossly over-valued the former. Second, there was the cost of moving and rehousing on Russian soil those divisions of the Red Army formerly based in East Germany. Through being financed by government-borrowing rather than by taxation, German reunification forced up world interest rates with world-wide deflationary consequences. In the case of the UK, the deflationary influences were magnified by its ill-fated venture into the European Exchange Rate Mechanism with its currency having been pegged at an unrealistically and, ultimately, unsustainably high value.

One response to the current world recession has been a call for more protectionism. There are indications that, notwithstanding the recent GATT agreement, the major economies of the world stand poised today on the threshold of a return to protectionism inside super-national trading blocks, one in Europe, a second in North America, and a third in the Pacific basin.

Amidst and on top of all this economic turmoil, there are distinct signs of a deep and pervasive social malaise currently afflicting the affluent societies of the West. Some of the more notable symptoms include rapidly increasing crime rates, particularly violent crime committed by juveniles and young offenders, a breakdown of the traditional two-parent nuclear family, and the widespread use of drugs. There is evidence that there has been a significant weakening of the institutions of socialization and control, school and family. Meanwhile, low birth-rates within these countries, plus improved standards of health-care leading to longer life-expectancy, have and will continue to increase the proportion of the elderly within them. The steadily rising costs of maintaining a steadily ageing population have put and will continue to put enormous pressure upon the health and social services. The governments of these countries have been forced to intervene and will continue to be forced to intervene in these areas as harder and harder decisions require to be made.

The Soviet experiment might well have revealed communism to be not the right economic solution for modern industrialized societies. But much that has transpired in the West since the close of the Thatcher–Reagan era has served to raise doubts in the minds of many whether the liberal democratic capitalist alternative can do any better.

This form of order continues to have relatively few admirers in the West. This is so particularly among its academic elite. Although their opinions have very little *direct* influence on public opinion, they do exert considerable indirect effect and this in two main ways. First, they educate the main future opinion-formers in politics and the media. Second, they legitimize – if they are not themselves the source of – the policy prescriptions and outlook of the more directly influential classes. Grudging admission is given these days by nearly all academics, politicians, and branches of the mass media to the superior efficacy of the market over central planning for production and distribution. However, little else about capitalism is conceded to be of much worth, and much is found deficient.

Above all, three complaints against liberal democratic capitalism enjoy wide currency today in Western intellectual circles. Appeal is regularly made to these complaints by governments and political parties in support of anti-capitalist legislative measures. The first, and, in many ways, politically the most influential of these complaints, is that liberal democratic capitalism creates and perpetuates morally unjustifiable forms and degrees of economic inequality. It is claimed to do so, even when fairly extensive state-welfare provision is made. Allegedly indefensible degrees of inequality are held to obtain both between advanced capitalist societies and their poorer trading partners, as well as between the better-off and less well-off individual members of capitalist societies, including between the male and female members of such societies.

This is the prime complaint against capitalism levelled by those who in all other respects would consider themselves 'liberals' and enthusiastic supporters of the wide civil and political liberties associated with advanced Western liberal democracies. Because of their support for the civil and political liberties enjoyed within these societies, it is customary for these critics of capitalism to refer to themselves and be referred to as liberals. However, I shall call them *modern liberals*. This is to distinguish them from another set of liberals who give more unreserved support to capitalism and whom I shall call *classical liberals*.

Variants of this first complaint can be found articulated in the writings of numerous contemporary Anglo-American philosophers. Most notable among these modern liberal critics of capitalism are John Rawls, Ronald Dworkin, Thomas Nagel, Kai Nielsen, and Ted Honderich, to name but the most prominent. It is also the complaint of those modern feminists, such as Susan Moller Okin and Alison Jaggar, who indict liberal capitalism for tolerating the perpetuation of traditional sex-roles said to disadvantage women.

A second widespread complaint is that liberal democratic capitalism severely damages, if not altogether destroys, the moral sensibility and culture of those who grow up and live within it. This it is alleged to do through destroying community in various forms. Some who make this claim also claim that it is only within such forms of association that human virtues are capable of being acquired and practised. Accordingly, it is part of this complaint against capitalist liberal democracy that it is said to impoverish the moral sensibility of its members. Variants of this complaint are made by all those who call themselves or have come to be called *communitarians*. Their most prominent members include Michael Sandel, Alisdair MacIntyre, Michael Walzer, and Charles Taylor.

The previous two complaints against liberal democratic capitalism are generally levelled by those on the left of the political spectrum. A third is levelled by those on the right. These critics of liberal capitalism are willing to accept the necessity and even the desirability of market institutions. However, so they maintain, the liberal democratic state is unable to create and preserve all of the various moral conditions required to sustain itself. Details of why this is so differ among Conservatives. Some, like Roger Scruton, argue that, through misguidedly liberal policies on immigration and cultural diversity, capitalist liberal democracy undermines the cultural unity needed for maintaining patriotic allegiance towards it on the part of its citizens. Others, like John Gray, argue that allegiance is undermined by the strictly limited government of liberal capitalism in other ways. Such a form of order is unable to win or preserve the allegiance of all those unable to support themselves by their own efforts on the market. Likewise, so it is said, this form of order is unable to guarantee a physical and cultural environment sufficiently rich in the public goods of culture as to provide members with what they need for civilized and commodious living. For a society to be able to satisfy the basic needs of all members, as well as their needs for such public goods, there is need for a state far more extensive than that advocated by classical liberals.

The purpose of the present book is to decide between classical liberals and their contemporary opponents. To reach an informed decision, it will be necessary to examine the case for and against the form of society which classical liberals recommend. The order in which I propose to carry out my enquiry is as follows. Chapter 2 presents the classical liberal case for capitalism and minimal government. Chapter 3 examines the critique mounted of it by modern liberals in the name of equality. Chapter 4 considers the communitarian critique, and Chapter 5 the conservative critique. In the case of all three sets of critics, it will be my intention to demonstrate that none of their complaints stands up to critical scrutiny.

It would be hard to exaggerate the practical importance of my conclusion. The world today is full of problems. Everyone agrees with that. How we go about seeking to solve them will ultimately be governed by our understanding of their causes. Whether our attempts succeed in resolving them or only make matters worse will depend upon whether we are correct in our diagnosis of their causes. Many of the world's problems are alleged to be caused by liberal capitalism of the sort advocated by classical liberals. These range from inner-city depravity, such as drugs, pornography and violent crime, to poverty in the third world, dangerous and virulent forms of nationalism and xenophobia, racism, the oppression of women, and environmental pollution. All are said to be beyond redress within the current framework of liberal democratic capitalist polities. In the sixth and concluding chapter, I shall briefly review these problems. I shall argue that, insofar as contemporary societies are afflicted with such problems, it is because these societies conform too closely to the nostrums of modern as opposed to classical liberalism. The solution is to be found by society recovering its path towards liberty as classical liberals understood it.

2 Classical Liberalism

2.1 THE FUNDAMENTAL PROBLEM OF POLITICAL PHILOSOPHY

Which form of political organization of society is best? This is the fundamental question of political philosophy. Beginning with Plato, the history of the subject may rightly to be regarded as nothing else than a prolonged – and, doubtless, unending – meditation on the question.

Different answers have been proffered at different times. And, not only at different times. In every age, philosophers have held different opinions on the subject. Despite all this diversity, on a very closely related issue there has always prevailed a surprisingly high degree of consensus among philosophers. This related question is that of the appropriate measure or criterion for deciding on the relative merits of different forms of political order. On this question, a large number among the most eminent political philosophers have all shared approximately the same conception. This is that the appropriate measure is the degree to which the different forms of societal order facilitate the well-being or happiness of a society's members.

The earliest and best-known written work of political philosophy is Plato's *Republic*. In this work, Plato undertakes to describe the form of the perfect political order. He does this by means of undertaking a sustained thought-experiment in which he constructs a perfect society in his imagination. In the course of this construction, Plato makes plain that, in his view, the decisive consideration in determining the merits of a form of political order is its conduciveness to the happiness of its members. Plato writes

> Our purpose in founding our state was . . . to promote the happiness . . . so far as possible of the whole community. . . . We are . . . trying to construct what we think is a happy community by securing the happiness . . . of the whole. . . . Our object is . . . happiness . . . in the community as a whole. . . . If it is, . . . our state will be built on the right basis, and, as it grows, we can leave each class to enjoy the share of happiness its nature permits.[1]

A similar view is endorsed by Plato's one-time pupil, Aristotle. In his *Politics*, Aristotle writes

> Let us consider what is the purpose of a state. . . . Man is by nature a political animal. And, therefore, men even when they do not require one

another's help, desire to live together; not but that they are also brought together by their common interests in proportion as they severally attain to any measure of well-being. This is certainly the chief end, both of individuals and states.[2]

The seventeenth-century British philosopher, Thomas Hobbes, is rightly considered by many to be the father of modern political philosophy. *Leviathan*, his *magnum opus*, espouses a similar view to that espoused by Plato and Aristotle on the proper purpose of government. The purpose of political society is to advance the happiness of its members. Hobbes writes

The office of the sovereign, (be it a monarch or an assembly,) consisteth in the end for which he was trusted with the sovereign power, namely the procuration of *the safety of the people*. . . . But by safety here is not meant a bare preservation, but also all other contentments of life, which every man by lawfull industry, without danger, or hurt to the community shall acquire to himself.[3]

A similar opinion is espoused by John Locke in his *Second Treatise of Government*, subtitled 'An essay concerning the origin, extent, and end of civil government'. In this work, Locke writes

The *end of civil society* [is] to avoid, and remedy those inconveniences of the state of nature . . . .[4] The only way whereby anyone divests himself of his natural liberty, and *puts on the bonds of civil society* is by agreeing with other men to join together and unite into a community, for their comfortable, safe, and peaceful living one amongst another, in a secure enjoyment of their properties, and a greater security against any that are not of it. . . .[5] The *legislative* power of every commonwealth in all forms of government . . . are to govern by *promulgated established laws* . . . *[which] ought to be designed* for *no other end but* the good of the people.[6]

Nearly one hundred years later, the same position was endorsed by Adam Smith, when he observed that 'all constitutions of government . . . are valued only in proportion as they tend to promote the happiness of those who live under them. This is their sole use and end.'[7] Much the same opinion was expressed by Adam Smith's contemporary, Adam Ferguson who, in his *Essay on the History of Civil Society*, stated that 'the happiness of individuals is the great end of civil society'.[8]

A century after Adam Smith and Adam Ferguson the same view finds expression in the political writings of Henry Sidgwick. In his *Elements of Politics*, Sidgwick wrote

The true standard and criterion by which right legislation is to be distinguished from wrong is conduciveness to the general 'good' or 'welfare' ... interpret[ing] the 'good' or 'welfare' of the community to mean, in the last analysis, the happiness of the individual human beings who compose the community, provided we take into account not only the human beings who are actually living but those who are to live hereafter.[9]

It would be folly to suggest that, in considering which form of political order is best, no philosopher has ever appealed to any other consideration besides the degree to which each different political form promotes the well-being of society's members. The pedigree of the view, however, is sufficiently impressive to make it a suitable place from which to start our enquiry. It is, then, by appeal to some such broad criterion that I propose to attempt to answer this fundamental question of political philosophy in the present study.

2.2 THE CLASSICAL LIBERAL SOLUTION: THE SYSTEM OF NATURAL LIBERTY

The purpose of the present book is to examine the credentials for being considered best one particular form of societal organization. This form was that first clearly delineated and advocated in the modern period by those political philosophers who have come to be called *classical liberals*. These include such thinkers as Adam Smith, David Ricardo, and Jeremy Bentham. It is also customary to include within the tradition such figures as David Hume, the two Mills, Senior, Dicey and Herbert Spencer. After falling into almost complete intellectual disrepute towards the end of the nineteenth century, classical liberalism was rescued from oblivion and revived in the twentieth century by such notable thinkers as Ludwig von Mises and Friedrich Hayek. The revival has spawned a whole spate of more recent thinkers inaccurately and now somewhat anachronistically known as the 'new right'. Included here are such figures as Robert Nozick, Loren Lomasky and Jan Narveson. In the next two sections, I shall seek to provide an outline of this form of order and of the main arguments that have been advanced on behalf of it.

At bottom, what distinguishes from all others that form of societal order which classical liberals maintain best for all human beings is the magnitude of the measure of liberty which it accords its sane adult members. This form of polity uniquely grants them the liberty to do whatever they want, provided no one but, at most, themselves is harmed by their doing it.

Following Adam Smith, I shall call this societal form *the system of natural liberty*.[10] Smith describes it as follows

> Every man, as long as he does not violate the laws of justice, is left perfectly free to pursue his own interest his own way.... The sovereign has only three duties to attend to ... : first, the duty of protecting the society from the violence and invasion of other independent societies; secondly, the duty of protecting, as far as possible, every member of the society from the justice or oppression of every other member of it; and, thirdly, the duty of erecting and maintaining certain public works and certain public institutions [such as ports and roads], which it can never be for the interest of any individual, or small number of individuals, to erect and maintain.... though it may frequently do much more than repay it to a great society.[11]

For brevity's sake, I shall call any political society which exemplifies this form of order a *liberal polity*. By *liberty*, in this context, I mean the *absence* of any legal or other form of deliberately imposed human restraint or impediment designed to prevent some person or persons from doing something. The most notable of such forms of restraint and impediment are, first, actual physical restraint, such as being tied up, handcuffed, or imprisoned, and, second, the threat of legal or other penalties, if some possible act is carried out (or not carried out).

The absence of any form of restraint or impediment standing in the way of an individual performing some particular act by no means suffices to render that individual able to perform that act. Suppose neither the state nor anyone else seeks to stop me from doing something. I still might not be able to do that thing. In these circumstances, I would possess the liberty but not the power or ability to do the thing in question. For example, I am currently at liberty – but am, nonetheless, unable – to run a mile in four minutes. Likewise, I am at liberty, but unable due to shortage of funds, to purchase a penthouse on Park Avenue.

Similarly, in order for members of a society to enjoy that measure of liberty which a liberal polity would accord them, something more is required than that there should be no laws prohibiting them from performing acts which harm no one but themselves. In addition, there is need of laws which are effectively enforced that prohibit members from engaging in acts which either restrict the liberty of other members or otherwise harm them.

Why do classical liberals maintain the system of natural liberty to be more conducive than any other form of societal order to the well-being or happiness of members of a society? In essence, classical liberals do so on the basis of two other claims that they make. The first is a doctrine which we might call *individualism with respect to ends*.[12] This doctrine is to the effect that, ultimately, each sane adult is the final authority as to which forms of activity and experience augment and which diminish his or her own individual happiness. Others may correctly think that some individual would greatly enjoy an activity or experience which that individual has so far not tried, or has tried but so far found unenjoyable, and which, perhaps, in consequence the individual mistakenly believes he or she would not enjoy if they were now to try it. However, all these opinions of others are corrigible. The ultimate arbiter of whether any activity or experience itself does or does not add to or diminish the happiness of an individual is that individual him or herself. An activity (or experience) augments the happiness of an individual if and only if it is one which that individual, on full reflection, would be pleased to have engaged in (or had), notwithstanding full knowledge of the consequences and opportunity costs of so doing.

The second doctrine on which classical liberals base their claim that the system of natural liberty is the form of societal order most conducive to the happiness of society's members may be called *individualism with respect to means*. This doctrine is to the effect that, within the limits imposed by the principle which forbids any individual to harm another, the happiness of each sane adult is best promoted through each such individual being accorded the liberty to pursue it as he or she pleases.

Why individualism with respect to ends and means jointly underwrites the system of natural liberty will best become apparent after we have seen why, when individuals are granted such a measure of liberty, one institution will necessarily arise. This is the institution of private property. Individuals were only thought by classical liberals to be the best judges of how to advance their own individual happiness against a background in which it was assumed they would enjoy the right to acquire, hold, and bequeath private property. It was because the system of natural liberty uniquely enabled a society's members to enjoy these property rights that classical liberals thought this system the one most conducive to the happiness of its members.

2.3   WHY LIBERTY IMPLIES PROPERTY

Whenever sane adult human beings are accorded the liberty to do what they want, provided they act innocuously, one major institution will be bound to develop. This is the institution of *private property*. The reason is as follows.

In order for the members of a society to be accorded that measure of liberty which a liberal polity accords its members, they must be protected against interference by others with their exercise of it. Imagine there is, as yet, no property in a society. Suppose an individual member took hold of some material thing, or used it for some purpose which involved or depended upon enjoying *indefinite exclusive use of that thing*. Say, for example, an individual were to *homestead* a portion of land which previously had neither been homesteaded by anyone else, nor used for any purpose which involved or required the indefinite exclusive use of it. Suppose, further, that taking hold of this land in this way does not worsen the lives of anyone else. That is, suppose that its becoming subject to the exclusive indefinite use by that person does not render the lives of anyone else worse than they were before, nor any worse than they would have been were people unable in this fashion to appropriate previously unowned things. In such circumstances, an individual who takes hold of a portion of land (or of any other material thing) in this way acts within the bounds of the measure of liberty accorded him in a liberal polity. Hence, in such a polity, individuals must be permitted to engage in such acts. More than that. Having so taken hold of that portion of land (or other item), any subsequent act by anyone else which deprives the original proprietor of exclusive use of whatever he had appropriated must count as an instance of harming the original proprietor. For any such act of deprivation frustrates the intention with which the item in question was appropriated originally.

Not only that. Consider any item which any member of society takes into their possession through original appropriation of it, or through being given it by its original or some subsequent proprietor of it. A liberal polity is one that protects the liberty of its members to do whatever they want that does not harm others. Consequently, such a form of polity must prohibit and seek to prevent anyone depriving any member, who is a proprietor of any material item, of the liberty to use or dispose of that item innocuously. This is because any attempt by anyone to deprive the proprietor of that liberty would frustrate the intent with which the proprietor either originally appropriated that item, or else subsequently received it from some previous proprietor of it. This, in effect, amounts to a liberal polity having to acknowledge and enforce property rights in all material things, including land, that their members have taken hold of or accepted in this way. In a liberal polity, the original person to take hold of anything previously unowned, for a purpose which involves or requires indefinite exclusive control of it, must be recognized as its rightful *owner*. The item must be regarded in a liberal society as the *legitimate private property* of that individual. Consequently, the necessity of a society's having to acknowledge and enforce legal rights to fully bequeathable private property is a natural and inevitable corollary of its according to its sane adult members that measure of liberty which a liberal polity accords them.

A possible objection can be anticipated to this derivation of property rights from the measure of liberty that is accorded to the members of a liberal polity. It might be claimed that other people are harmed by someone taking hold of a previously unowned object for a purpose which involves their exclusive indefinite use of it. 'Surely, others are harmed', it might be said, 'by the fact that they are no longer at liberty to use the object whereas, before it was taken hold of, they were.'

However, the appropriation by an individual of some item previously unappropriated by anyone else need not necessarily have harmed these others through their no longer being at liberty to use the items appropriated. The lives of these others need not necessarily have been made any worse than they would have been had they continued to be at liberty to use these items. As has been convincingly argued by both Robert Nozick and David Gauthier,[13] it is extremely implausible to suppose that the life of anyone has ever been made worse as a result of people having been at liberty to appropriate things previously unappropriated by anyone. Suppose no one were at liberty to appropriate previously unappropriated objects, including land through homesteading it. No one would have had anything like as much incentive as the liberty to appropriate provides them for improving things through expending their labour upon them. For example, if homesteading land did not confer a title to it, no one would be secure in being able to enjoy the benefits of any improvement they might have cared to make to such land. It is true that, when someone appropriates some previously unappropriated item, other people are no longer at liberty to use or appropriate that object for themselves. But the life of an individual is not necessarily worsened in ceasing to be at liberty to use or appropriate some item as a result of someone else having appropriated it.

Someone's appropriating an item unowned by anyone else need not make others worse-off than they were before this act of appropriation took place. Before it took place, the item no more belonged to these others than it did after. As a result of an item's being appropriated by someone else, these others may no longer be at liberty to use the item as before they were. In the case of land, for example, they might cease to be able to walk across it. But the appropriation of the land need not have harmed them. All it has necessarily done is merely prevent them from being able to benefit themselves from using it as they previously were able to benefit themselves by using it. It is an open question whether their being prevented from being able so to benefit themselves in this way, as a result of the land's having been appropriated by another, should count as an instance of their having been harmed. Whether it should depends on which of the following two possible alternative forms of societal order better serves their well-being: that in which they remain at liberty to use land (or other natural resources) as they did before, without appropriating any – because no one enjoys the liberty to appropriate anything; or that in which people are at liberty to appropriate previously unappropriated land or other natural resources. I have argued above that the life prospects of people are better served within the second rather than within the first of these forms of order. A liberal polity, therefore, must inexorably generate a system of private property rights based upon the homesteading principle.

Such a system of private property rights might be thought to constitute a very unpromising basis from which to construct a case for the thesis that this form of polity is best for all human beings in terms of best promoting their well-being. But I now wish to rehearse the classical liberal case on behalf of this view.

On behalf of their preferred form of social order, classical liberals advance arguments of two sorts, *economic* and *non-economic*. The *economic arguments* are designed to prove that no form of societal order besides the liberal one better enables its members to acquire and enjoy possession of such material goods and services as they each might want for themselves, their loved ones, and for whomever else they wished to benefit. The *non-economic arguments* are intended to establish the corresponding thesis in respect of what, following Franz Brentano,[14] I shall call *spiritual goods*. By this expression, I intend to designate such non-material goods as people desire for their own sake. The most prominent of these are knowledge, love and aesthetic pleasure. The chief spiritual goods relevant to our discussion are those for which a necessary condition is freedom of thought and expression, namely, freedom of religious worship and of voluntary association. I shall now rehearse each of these arguments.

2.4 THE ECONOMIC CASE FOR LIBERTY

Human beings associate with one another in a number of different ways and for a number of different purposes. In all cases, they do so for the sake of certain advantages which each associate expects to derive from so doing. The various concrete forms of association fall into one or other of three different categories. The first is that of the family. The second category includes all those voluntary associations which together comprise what is often called the sphere of *civil society*. The third category of association is that of political society itself or the state. Before rehearsing the economic case for the liberal polity, I shall now briefly discuss all three main kinds of association in turn.

A family is formed by a man and woman cohabiting and having and raising children together. The advantages which those who form families together expect to derive from so doing are those which derive from sharing their lives with one another and having children. Typically, the most important of these are the love, friendship, intimacy and companionship that arises between a cohabiting couple and between them and any children they might have and raise.

It is for the sake of other sorts of advantage besides those associated with family life that human beings establish and engage in extra-familial forms of association. With one notable exception, all these various forms of extra-familial association fall within the domain of *civil society*. The exception is the *state* or political community itself. Rather than its falling within civil society, the state is the domain within which civil society itself falls.

Civil society is not so much some one single extra-familial form of association. It is, rather, the sum of private voluntary associations that develop between individuals beyond the spheres of their respective families. All these arise spontaneously, and are maintained through voluntary agreements between individuals, when they are at liberty to form them. Beyond the expected benefits of family life, there are many different purposes for which human beings voluntarily associate with one another. Among the constituent associations of civil society, some are created for the specific purpose of producing or distributing material goods and services. There are many other purposes besides this one for which extra-familial voluntary associations are created to secure. Examples of such forms of association include churches, synagogues, clubs, learned societies, schools, universities and political parties. With the exception of the state itself, there is, typically, no single association to which every member of any society belongs. However, typically, every member of any society will belong to a number of extra-familial association(s) to which many other members will also belong.

Besides the family and all the various forms of association that fall within the domain of civil society, there is a third distinct kind of association. This is the *state* or *polity*. A *polity* is a form of association all of whose members recognize the same individual, or body of individuals, as having authority to make and enforce laws governing them while they remain within a certain territory. The individual or body of individuals so recognized constitutes the sovereign or government. The type of association so formed constitutes a political community or state or polity.

Why do individuals form, remain in, and join, political communities? As with the other sorts of association into which they enter, they do so for the sake of advantages they expect to derive not otherwise obtainable. In the case of the state, the primary such advantage is protection from aggression both from non-members and from fellow members of that state.

No member of any society can for long continue as its sovereign or head of government without enjoying the consent of the majority of members of that society. Where such majority consent is absent, sooner or later those in charge of the government will be replaced. The well-being of a society's members is liable to be best served when its form of organization permits the peaceful and orderly replacement of those in charge of government, when they no longer command the support of the majority. Consequently, in order for it to be the best form of social organization, a liberal polity will need to be a democracy. This is in the limited sense that the leadership of the body that is the government will have to be selected by means of periodic democratic election. Latter-day classical liberals, such as Hayek and von Mises, therefore, believe the best form of liberal polity must be one in which those who form the government are appointed by means of periodic democratic election. This is to allow those who are governed to replace peacefully those who govern them should they find their governors unsatisfactory.

The economic case for the liberal polity is based on the material benefits that each member may expect to derive from those forms of association in civil society that are created and maintained for the purpose of producing and distributing material goods and services. The specific type of benefit which anyone who enters into any such association expects to gain from so doing is some share of the increased productivity of labour that such forms of association make possible. In sum, everyone who enters into any such form of association does so in the expectation of being able thereby to obtain, either for themselves and for others about whom they care, more in the way of desired material goods and services than they otherwise expect to be able to obtain.

These forms of association increase the productivity of the labour of their participants by facilitating a *division of labour* between the associates, and between them and their trading partners. This division of labour increases the productivity of labour by facilitating an ever greater degree of specialization, leading to ever improving technique. When individuals are accorded that measure of liberty which a liberal polity accords them, they invariably can and do end up much better able to supply themselves, and those about whom they care, with what they want in material goods and services. This claim is subject to two provisos.

The first is that, for each form of association specializing in producing one type of good or service, it must be possible for its associates to exchange what they produce for goods and services produced by others in ways that both sets of parties find advantageous to themselves. Accordingly, *trading* between individuals or companies (or between an individual and a company) constitutes a distinct type of informal association between individuals within civil society.

The second proviso is that individuals can expect to benefit from entering into any of these associations only when they are at liberty to leave them. Only when they enjoy liberty of exit can each associate be assured of being able to command a larger share of the increased productivity of their labour than they can otherwise obtain. The measure of liberty which a liberal polity accords its members includes the liberty to form contracts which permit such exit under mutually agreed terms. That a liberal polity accords its members such a measure of liberty constitutes a major part of the classical liberal thesis that such a polity is best for all human beings.

Besides the increases which derive from specialization, there is another major way in which the productivity of labour can be increased. This is by increasing the ratio of capital to labour. By *capital*, I mean all those goods, such as equipment, machines, and tools, used in the process of producing other goods. The productivity of labour increases with the quantity of capital available for use by labour. These capital goods can be produced only at the cost of the producers of them forgoing leisure or else of more immediate consumption. Individuals forgo leisure or more immediate consumption to produce and deploy capital goods only if they stand to benefit from doing so. They benefit only if they are able to keep, or decide on the manner of disposal of, some portion of the extra yield of labour made possible by the capital goods they have made available. Individuals have incentive to forgo leisure or earlier consumption for the sake of creating capital goods only if two conditions hold. The first is that they enjoy security of possession in these goods, as well as in whatever benefit they can innocuously obtain by means of them. The second is that they are at liberty to make use of their capital available to others on mutually agreed terms. A major part of the classical liberal case for the liberal polity is that the measure of liberty which it accords its members uniquely satisfies these two conditions.

Whenever these conditions obtain, a society is liable to develop an economy based on capital accumulation and wage labour. It is because of this that, as von Mises has observed, 'a society in which liberal principles are put into effect is usually called a capitalist society, and the condition of that society, capitalism'.[15]

We may summarize the economic argument as follows. Any polity that accords to its members that measure of personal liberty which a liberal polity does must acknowledge and uphold a legal right to private property. In consequence of its according this measure of liberty, this form of political association will enable its members to enjoy a far higher material standard of living than they would otherwise be able to do.

2.5 THE NON-ECONOMIC CASE FOR LIBERTY

'A good life involves more than material goods. Man does not live by bread alone. All you have so far succeeded in showing, if anything, is that a liberal polity enables its members to obtain innocuously a stock of material goods and services larger than any which they might otherwise have been able to obtain. But is not such a type of polity only going to be best for those who have no higher aspirations than to acquire material things and services rendered by others? Isn't such a society best only for philistines or swine?'

The answer is that this is not so. Classical liberals maintain that no form of polity better enables human beings to enjoy spiritual goods than does the liberal one. This is a somewhat neglected part of the classical liberal case for the liberal polity. Among the chief spiritual goods for which they make this claim are such goods as knowledge, love, virtue, and aesthetic enjoyment.

To see in what way the liberal polity is said to do this, consider, first, religion. Every individual must want – or feel constrained in conscience – to practise (or not practise) religion in some manner. In either case, every individual must, on reflection, prefer to possess, rather than to lack, the liberty to practise (or not practise) religion in whichever manner they want or feel constrained to practise (or not practise) it.

This liberty to practice (or to refrain from practising) religion is an indispensable condition of that spiritual good which consists in living in accordance with one's conscience. It is a liberty about which people feel passionately. It is a liberty for which historically people have often been willing to die. Provided the form of religion – or irreligion – they wish to practice is not one that involves their harming others, the liberal polity provides everyone with such a measure of liberty.

By virtue of the measure of liberty which it accords its members, a liberal polity must provide its members with the freedom to practise (or not practise) religion innocuously, according as they see fit. However, its doing so does not by itself suffice to establish that this form of polity best enables its members to practise religion or atheism, according to their own individual predilections. This is because people may be able to live in a form of polity which accords them the liberty to practise, or not practise, religion in the manner they would wish, without according this same liberty to anyone who follows a religious faith different to their own. Consequently, the fact that a liberal polity accords to all its members the liberty to practise the faith of their choice does not, by itself, establish that such a form of polity is best for every member.

Some might prefer to live in a form of polity which prohibited the practice of any other form of faith but their own! If this should be a very strong preference of theirs, they might prefer to live within an illiberal polity that permitted, or even required, the practice of only their own faith than to live in a polity which permitted everyone to practise the faith of their choice. For example, orthodox Jews might prefer to live in a society which prohibits any Jew from travelling on the sabbath, to living in one that not only permits any member not to travel on that day but also permits any member to travel on that day. Roman Catholics might prefer to live in a society in which no one is permitted to practise contraception than to live in one which merely permits its members to refrain from using contraception, but equally permits them to practise contraception.

A liberal polity, therefore, imposes a certain constraint upon religious practice. How do liberals justify this constraint? It must be admitted that there appear to be many people who, after full reflection, would prefer that only their own religion be allowed to be practised than that others be allowed to practise other forms of faith or atheism. However, these people are often resident in societies also populated by those who do not share their particular faith, or, indeed, any. In terms of deciding which form of polity best facilitates the happiness of these religious people, the alternatives between which they are compelled to choose are those that are feasible. It is almost certainly the case, that, where people of many different faiths and life-styles are already living together, the extension of religious tolerance to others is the price that each member must pay for being allowed to live according to their own particular faith. The measure of liberty which all members are accorded within a liberal polity allows everyone to practise or not practise religion according to their own lights.

Therefore, although there are some people who might, on full reflection, prefer to live in regimes in which only their own religion is tolerated than to live in ones which extend tolerance to many other faiths than theirs and to atheists, this does not invalidate the liberal claim. Where, either by choice or from necessity, such people live among others of different religious faiths or predilection to their own, the choice with which they are faced on the matter is not that between tolerance of other faiths besides their own or the hegemony of their own. Rather, it is between tolerance of other faiths or civil war. Historically speaking, it was in seventeenth-century England, and, then, only after a bloody civil war fought along religious lines, that it first became generally recognized in Europe that religious toleration was preferable for everyone to religious intolerance because of the civil dissension to which the latter inexorably led.[16]

With respect to all other forms of expression and activity, classical liberals maintain a similar case for tolerance of innocuous forms of expression and activity. Such tolerance is a condition of everyone's being able to obtain those spiritual goods which are of most importance to them.

Some might believe that everyone would be better off living in societies which prohibited certain forms of innocuous, but nonetheless morally wicked, conduct. However, unless such forms of conduct can be shown to be harmful to others besides those who engage in them, human beings should, on reflection, prefer to live in societies which permit such private harmless vices to those in which government is licensed to prohibit conduct on the grounds of its being wicked or dangerous to those who engage in it. The reason is this. Once governments are given the authority to restrict the liberty of some sane adults for what it considers their physical or moral welfare, there is no principled stopping point in terms of what governments will have authority to prohibit. The consequence will be that virtually anything which anyone holds of most value may become prohibited to them on grounds of its being judged immoral or dangerous to them. There are practically no forms of activity in which sane adults like to engage that others are not able to find reasons to condemn as morally or physically bad for those who engage in them. This ranges from drinking alcohol and smoking tobacco, to eating certain types of food, to not taking exercise, to taking too much, engaging in dangerous sports, practising certain religions, not practising any religion, reading books on science, etc. Unless government draws the line at only prohibiting conduct that harms others against their will, no member of society can be secure in being able to do or have anything they most want and value. Unless the line is drawn there, all members are in danger of having their government on moralistic or paternalistic grounds prohibit them from doing that which they most want to do, despite its harming no one but themselves and despite their knowledge of the risks involved. No one could, on reflection, prefer a life in which they were in danger of being subject to such restrictions on their liberty to one in which they were not. This is so, even if the price of their enjoying the liberty to live as they most want is having to tolerate the presence within their midst of victimless vices and imprudent action by others.

This, in essence, then, is the classical liberal case on behalf of the liberal polity as being that form of regime which is best for all human beings. It is not transparently obvious and will require elaboration and further elucidation in the chapters to come. There is, however, one possible objection to it which I should like to dispose of in the following and concluding section of the present chapter.

2.6   THE STARVING MAN IN THE LIBERAL POLITY

'How can the liberal polity possibly be the best form of polity for anyone who happened to be destitute within it? Such a polity makes no provision for them. The government in such a polity only undertakes to protect the life, liberty, and property of its members. It acknowledges no legal right on the part of anyone to be provided with succour in the event they are destitute. In order for some form of polity to be the best regime for all its members, it surely has to be one which guarantees succour to those who would otherwise be destitute. Consequently, the liberal polity cannot be best for all human beings.'

No single other consideration has done more than this to foster intellectual resistance to classical liberalism and antipathy to the form of social order recommended by it. By refusing to countenance welfare rights, classical liberalism is widely thought to fail to accommodate the needs and interests of those who, through no fault of their own, are destitute and unable to provide for themselves. What I shall now attempt to argue is that no single other objection to classical liberalism betrays a more profound misconception of the issues involved!

It is certainly true that the form of social organization which classical liberals claim best is one which would not provide its members with any legal right to welfare. By contrast, it would acknowledge every member as having a right to life, liberty and property. However, from the fact that a liberal polity does not acknowledge or confer upon all its members as having a legal right to welfare, it cannot be inferred that, within a liberal polity, those unable to provide for themselves innocuously would fare any less well than they would were they to enjoy such a legal right. Nor, from its not conferring or acknowledging such a right, can it be inferred that a liberal polity would not be entitled or required to hold *some* individuals legally responsible for the welfare of those unable to provide for themselves.

A government may acknowledge a legal right to welfare and announce an intent to take care of all those who cannot look after themselves. The existence of such a legal right and such an intent does not by itself guarantee, in practice, that there will be fewer destitute than there would have been had that polity been a purely liberal one and without any such right to welfare being acknowledged. It could well be that attempts by government to take care of the destitute – through acknowledging and administering legal rights to welfare – do not reduce the number or plight of the destitute but only exacerbate the problem. The mere existence of constitutional guarantees of support and succour for all in need does not guarantee such support and succour will be provided by the government to all in need of it. Likewise, the absence of such constitutional guarantees of support and succour does not guarantee that anyone will lack such support and succour.

Not only that. The existence of a state welfare apparatus designed to ensure a decent living is had by those unable to provide one for themselves does not necessarily increase the likelihood that a decent life will be had by those unable to provide for themselves. Despite the intent of the policy, it can have the effect of increasing the numbers of those unfortunates who find themselves needing such support.

'But are you suggesting that the state wash its hands of those unable to provide for themselves? Are you suggesting that the state must let them starve to death?'

The answer is that, in this area, it is vitally important to distinguish cases. Let us begin right at the beginning, with a new-born baby. Here, we have a human being unable to provide for itself. This is so, whether the baby is born healthy or congenitally disabled. Let us begin by supposing the baby is healthy. It will die unless cared for by someone. If a new-born is left to die, is this a case of its being harmed or merely of its not being benefited? Certainly, through not being cared for, its life would be worse than it would have been had it been cared for. However, whether anyone else may be said to have worsened the life of the new-born through failing to care for it depends on the circumstances of the case.

Consider, first, someone who is a perfect stranger to the baby. Suppose the mother dies in childbirth and the new-born baby survives. There it is, out in the fields, crying loudly next to the still-warm corpse of its mother. A stranger passes by. If the stranger fails to do anything to help the baby, will the stranger's failure to help have worsened the life of that baby? The stranger's failure to help the baby, I maintain, cannot be thought of as a case of worsening that baby's life as opposed simply to refraining from benefiting it.

The case where the life of a baby depends upon the assistance of a perfect stranger, however, is highly exceptional. I have begun by focusing on this extreme and highly atypical case to contrast it with another. This is where a mother survives the birth of her baby. Would its natural mother (and father) be worsening its life, if she (and he) failed to look after it in circumstances in which it depends for its survival on her (or his) care? There is an important difference between the relation in which the *natural parents* of a child stand towards their child and that in which perfect strangers stand to it. Unlike anyone else, a child's parents were causally responsible for having brought it into existence. This difference affects the issue as follows. Assume that, in the case of a particular new-born, there are only two options available for it. The first is for it not to have been conceived at all. The second is for it to have been conceived, brought to term, and then left to die upon birth. Although clearly new-borns are themselves incapable of reflecting on these options and choosing between them, it is not unreasonable to suppose that, *per impossibile*, were any new-born hypothetically faced with only these two options and invited to choose between them, after full reflection, the new-born would prefer not to have been born. Upon this assumption, it follows that any natural parent who avoidably leaves their new-born to die worsens its life in a way a stranger doesn't through failing to help it. For the parents, unlike the stranger, did something to cause the new-born to have this life less preferable than non-existence. Accordingly, a liberal polity is justified in compelling the natural parents of a child to provide for it, until such a time as that child becomes capable of providing for itself, or else a third party voluntarily assumes responsibility for it instead of the parents. This, then, is how a liberal polity could ensure that children are provided for other than by means of acknowledging universal welfare rights.

'But suppose a man and woman produce a child without being both able and willing to look after it, and suppose no one else is voluntarily willing to look after it?' To this, it may be replied that the couple would, then, be guilty of a serious offence. 'Yes, all very well and true. But this does not solve the problem of what is to happen in the case of such a child.' The answer is that it is extraordinarily difficult to envisage circumstances in which a couple have enough means of subsistence for their own survival but not enough for any child they have conceived. Moreover, since, as I have argued, bringing a human being into existence and then neglecting it with the result that it dies is tantamount to harming it, it follows that a liberal polity would be justified in threatening and imposing penalties on those who did. This would undoubtedly reduce the incidence of babies being born to couples unable or able but unwilling to look after them with their own resources.

Between the natural parents of a child and a perfect stranger to it, there are intermediate cases: notably, those who voluntarily assume responsibility for a child, or declare a willingness to do so, such as an orphanage or an adoption agency. If there exist agencies, such as orphanages, which have expressly indicated in advance a willingness to look after children in place of their natural parents (if the latter are unable or unwilling to care for them themselves), then, provided the lives which these agencies could make available to the children are ones that, on reflection, those children would prefer having had to having had none at all, then their natural parents do not worsen the lives of those children they have but fail to care for and which are cared for by these agencies.

'But what happens in the case of an adult who, through no fault of their own, has become unable to provide for themselves and there is no one willing to provide for him. Suppose, for example, that a farmer's estate and assets are destroyed by a hurricane and his insurance company has gone bust? Must he be left to die?'

Again, one is dealing with an extreme case. Normally, it should be possible, by means of saving or taking out insurance, for individuals to secure themselves against circumstances in which they are unable to look after themselves through accident, sickness, and old age. If someone possesses the opportunity to provide for such circumstances but fails to do so, society can hardly be accused of having failed to enable him to do so. In exceptional cases, an able-bodied person can become unable to provide for him or herself, and have no legal means of obtaining means of subsistence, for example, through appeal to charity. In such circumstances, that individual will have little option but to try and secure means of subsistence through some form of illegal action. Society will then have a right and duty to stop him with the minimum degree of necessary force. If people knew, in advance, that they would be liable for penalty if they were to become completely destitute, the incidence of indigence would be likely to fall considerably.

There is no easy solution to the problems of poverty and indigence. However, there is no case for supposing that the way these problems would be dealt with in a liberal polity would be any less humane than in a society in which legal rights to welfare were enshrined in the constitution. The course of Western societies that have acknowledged such rights does not inspire much confidence in them.

Although this takes care of problems associated with indigence, there are many other ways in which the classical liberal arguments for their favoured form of social order can be resisted. One is by claiming that the degrees of inequality which a liberal order generates and tolerates are morally unacceptable. In the next chapter we shall examine several versions of this way of resisting classical liberalism.

3 Modern Liberalism

3.1 MODERN VERSUS CLASSICAL LIBERALISM

No society has ever fully exemplified that form which classical liberals maintain is best. Classical liberal ideas greatly influenced the founding fathers of the USA in their design of its constitution. They also inspired much reform in Britain in the nineteenth century. However, today, neither society comes close to being a liberal polity as classical liberals conceive of one. Both contain far too much legislation and regulation restrictive of the liberty of members. Among such is all that which authorizes the government to impose taxes so as to create a far higher degree of material equality than would otherwise exist. All taxation for such redistributive purposes amounts to interference with what would otherwise be the spontaneous distributive outcome of the voluntary transactions between individuals. In the eyes of classical liberals, government acts other than innocuously when it compels one person to part with portions of what would otherwise be their own property for the sake of supplying benefits to others. This is so, despite such governmental activity being supposedly benevolent in intent. It worsens the lives of those compelled to pay these taxes. Such governmental redistribution undoubtedly receives the support of the mass of the electorate in such societies. But majority approval no more makes such taxation morally right than where what receives majority approval is the extermination or persecution of some ethnic or religious minority.

As remarked, the majority of the electorates of the liberal democracies are seemingly in favour of the egalitarian policies pursued within them. Nonetheless, it is almost certainly the case that electoral support for these policies would not be forthcoming without support for these policies being given by a large number, if not the overwhelming majority, of intellectuals and other opinion-formers in such societies. On the question of the effectiveness and equity of egalitarian forms of legislation, public opinion is very heavily influenced by that of political and social scientists and political philosophers. There currently exists a much higher degree of consensus among these latter groups than there has ever been before on the untenability of socialism as a possible form of organization. There is likewise much more consensus than there has ever been on the need for market institutions, including private ownership of the means of production. Despite this, it would be fair to say that, on the question of the moral propriety and wisdom of promoting more equality than is created by unimpeded market institutions, the consensus among political thinkers continues to be what it has been for most of this century, certainly since the Great Depression and the New Deal. This consensus is that the egalitarian legislative measures and policies adopted by governments since the beginning of the century have been both effective in improving the life-prospects of the less well-off and equitable. In other words, it would be fair to say that classical liberals are very much in a minority among the intelligentsia of present-day liberal societies.

Although by no means *classical* liberals, the overwhelming majority of present-day intellectuals in the Western democracies would consider themselves liberal on issues other than those connected with equality, such as personal morality and life-style. Indeed, the term 'liberal' has now come to stand in some of these countries, notably, the USA, for someone who supports egalitarian policies. The classical liberal view has come to be called 'conservative'. In order to keep clear the difference between the two outlooks, and not to award the term exclusively to either position, I have chosen to refer to the two positions by the expressions *classical* and *modern* liberalism. The purpose of this chapter is to decide between these two kinds of liberalism. Since they are largely agreed on matters connected with civil liberty, I shall focus on their major point of disagreement, namely, the equity and effectiveness of egalitarian public policy.

Modern liberals are welfare-state liberals. They also tend to be in favour of equal opportunities legislation in all its various forms. Some go further by favouring affirmative action and reverse discrimination in education and employment. These involve giving preferential treatment to members of previously disadvantaged minorities so as to improve their life-prospects. In all this, modern liberals are motivated by an over-arching commitment to an ideal of equality alien to and incompatible with classical liberalism. This is not to say that classical liberals have no place or regard for equality. This is far from so. But equality, for classical liberals, means primarily 'equality before the law'. By this term, classical liberals understand that the law recognize each member of society as enjoying an equal standing, and hence an equal right to life, to liberty and to acquire and enjoy secure possession of property.

Modern liberals take exception to those forms and degrees of inequality that would spontaneously arise among members of society when they are accorded a measure of liberty which permits them to do what they want provided what they do does not worsen the lives of others. Classical liberals find such inequalities unobjectionable and innocuous. What arguments do modern liberals advance in support of their opposition to such forms of inequality and how convincing are they? These are the questions to which we now turn. I shall consider, in turn, several arguments against the liberal polity advanced by prominent modern liberals in recent years. My conclusion will be that none of these arguments is sound.

3.2 JUSTICE AS FAIRNESS, NATURAL ENDOWMENT AND DESERT

No modern philosopher has done more than John Rawls to promote the egalitarian outlook characteristic of modern liberalism. This he did with the publication in 1971 of his much-heralded book, *A Theory of Justice*.[1] No other modern work of political philosophy has attracted anything like the same degree of critical acclaim or attention. A particular conception of society underlies Rawls' theory.

> [S]ociety is a cooperative venture for mutual advantage . . . , a more or less self-sufficient association of persons who in their relations to one another recognize certain rules . . . [which] specify a system of cooperation designed to advance the good of those taking part in it. . . .[2]

Rawls' theory is intended to provide an account of the conditions that must be satisfied by the fundamental political and economic institutions of a modern constitutional democracy in order that they jointly provide a system of fair cooperation for its members. The subject of the theory, therefore, is what Rawls calls *the basic structure of society*.[3] By this, he means all the major institutions of a society. The basic structure, thus, includes the political constitution as well as the principal economic and social institutions, such as private property and the monogamous family. This basic structure distributes fundamental rights and duties and determines the division among the members of society of the advantages gained from social cooperation. As Rawls notes, what he means by the basic structure of a society exerts an enormous influence upon the life-prospects of its individual members. These are 'what they can expect to be and how well they can hope to do'.[4] Rawls' theory is intended to stipulate what conditions must be satisfied by that set of institutions comprising the basic structure of a society in order for the advantages created by the social cooperation between its members to be distributed among them fairly.

At bottom, Rawls' theory consists of two principles, together with their supporting rationale. The specific conception of justice which the principles jointly supply is called by Rawls 'justice as fairness'. The first principle specifies the conditions which the chief political institutions must satisfy to be just. The second specifies the conditions which must be satisfied by the chief economic institutions to qualify for the same accolade. In his most recent formulation of the two principles, Rawls specifies them as follows.

> 1. *Each person has an equal right to a fully adequate scheme of equal basic rights and liberties, which scheme is compatible with a similar scheme for all.*
>
> 2. *Social and economic inequalities are to satisfy two conditions: first, they must be attached to offices and positions open to all under fair equality of opportunity; and second, they must be to the greatest benefit of the least advantaged members of society.*[5]

On the issue of how much civil, religious and political liberty members of society should have, classical and modern liberals are not far apart. Consequently, something like Rawls' first principle is common ground between them. Where they disagree with one another is over what considerations should govern the assignment of benefits and rewards to different offices and positions, as well as what should govern the methods to be used in appointing individuals to these offices. These matters are addressed by Rawls' second principle. As can be seen, this principle is itself composed of two separate ones. The first of these Rawls calls *the principle of fair equality of opportunity*, the second *the difference principle*.

Rawls makes two claims in support of his conception of justice. The first is that it accords with our most settled and considered moral judgements. The second is that, when unable to gain any advantage over others by means of selecting principles which specially favour themselves, everyone would select Rawls' two principles in preference to any others as the underlying principles which should govern the design of the basic structure of society. We shall now examine the arguments advanced by Rawls in support of each of these two claims. Unless they provide good reason to accept at least one of them, his theory of justice will lack support. Hence, his theory will not provide reason to condemn a liberal polity for the inequalities it permits.

Classical liberals need have no quarrel with his first principle of justice. Consequently, we shall confine our attention to the arguments for his two claims as applied on behalf of his second principle. We begin by examining the considerations which Rawls adduces in support of the claim that the second of his two principles is in accord with our most considered moral judgements.

In support of his second principle of justice, Rawls' first claim is that any form of social order that fails to accord with it must offend a deep-seated moral intuition we have about desert. The alleged moral intuition is that it is unjust for one person to enjoy better life-prospects than others who are no less deserving than the first person, unless the first person's enjoying these more favourable life-prospects is to the over-all advantage of the least well-off of these others.

Rawls invites his readers to agree that they share this moral intuition by arguing as follows. First, he considers a form of order which satisfies only his first principle. Following the lead of Adam Smith, he calls such a form of order *the system of natural liberty*. This form of order corresponds roughly with what we understand as a liberal polity. It differs only in that discrimination in employment on grounds of sex or race is not permitted.

Does such a system accord with our considered moral judgements? Rawls maintains it does not for the following reason. Assume that, within the system of natural liberty, as envisaged by Rawls, life-prospects are a function of income, and that income is a function of marketable skills and willingness to use them. In such a form of order, those able to acquire the most marketable skills will enjoy the best life-prospects. But this can often be those whose parents have been able to provide their children with the best education.

The system of natural liberty, thus, permits different individuals possessing similar natural talents and willingness to use them to acquire different qualifications, and hence to acquire different life-prospects through receiving dissimilar education. Accordingly, the system of natural liberty permits some to acquire better life-prospects than others on the basis of 'social circumstances and such chance contingencies as accident and good fortune'.[6] Of differential life-prospects so acquired by otherwise similarly endowed individuals, Rawls remarks 'intuitively, the most obvious injustice of the system of natural liberty is that it permits distributive shares to be improperly influenced by these factors so arbitrary from a moral point of view'.[7]

It is in order to eliminate the influence of such morally arbitrary factors as the better education that can be purchased for their child by wealthy parents that Rawls introduces his principle of fair equality of opportunity. Fair equality of opportunity is designed to ensure that those of similar natural talents and similar willingness to use them should have similar life-chances. Any distribution of life-prospects to individuals arising in the absence of fair equality of opportunity is unfair.[8]

When supplemented by the principle of fair equality of opportunity, the system of natural liberty becomes what Rawls calls a system of *liberal equality*. According to Rawls, this system still fails to accord with our considered moral judgements. For life-prospects are still determined within

it by differences between individuals that, claims Rawls, we must agree
to be arbitrary from a moral point of view. These differences are those of
natural talent.[9] It is in order to 'mitigate the arbitrary effects of the natural
lottery',[10] as regards the distribution of both natural talent as well as of
favourable family background, that Rawls introduces the difference principle. The system that results from combining the difference principle with
that of fair equality Rawls calls that of *democratic equality*.[11] The difference principle is justified, therefore, in the same manner as was the principle of fair equality of opportunity. For the basic structure of society not
to satisfy the difference principle, claims Rawls, is for that structure to be
at variance with our considered moral judgement. The specific moral judgement with which the offending social structures are said not to accord is
that it is unjust for those of equal desert to enjoy unequal life-prospects,
unless such an inequality works to the advantage of those enjoying the less
favourable life-prospects. Rawls observes

> No one deserves his greater natural capacity nor merits a more favour-
> able starting place in society. . . . [W]e are led to the difference principle
> if we wish to set up the social system so that no one gains or loses from
> his arbitrary place in the distribution of natural assets or his initial posi-
> tion in society without giving or receiving compensating advantages in
> return.[12]

> In justice as fairness, men . . . undertake to avail themselves of the acci-
> dents of nature and social circumstances only when doing so is for the
> common benefit. The two principles of justice are a fair way of meeting
> the arbitrariness of fortune.[13]

It is clear from what Rawls writes that there is only one sort of difference between individuals which morally justifies their enjoying different
life-prospects. This is differences in degree of merit or desert. Rawls says
little about what he considers makes one person deserving of better prospects than another. However, it is clear he thinks no one deserves better
life-prospects than others merely for having been born with greater than
average natural talents, or for having been born into a wealthier family
than others.

Beyond claiming that they accord with our considered moral judgements, Rawls makes a second claim on behalf of his two principles of
justice. They would, claims Rawls, be chosen above all others by anyone
required to choose principles governing the design of the basic structure
of their society when required to choose impartiality. By 'impartiality'
is meant choosing principles without being able to tailor choice so as to

specially favour oneself. Rawls argues for this second claim by means of a thought experiment. Suppose people had to select principles of justice without knowing any specific facts about themselves, such as what natural talents they had or from which social class they came. Suppose all they knew about themselves was that they had interests which would be served by their having more rather than less of what Rawls calls *social primary goods*. These are goods, such as wealth, which are instrumentally good for any purposes one might have. Rawls argues that, if people were unaware of their own specific identity, and forced to choose principles governing the design of their social structure, then they would have no conceivable reason for selecting any principles other than his two. For no one prefers a smaller than a larger stock of primary goods. Hence, in such a choice-situation everyone would choose that their society provide strict equality in terms of maximum equal liberty and in terms of the distribution of primary goods, except where an unequal distribution of primary goods improves the life-prospects of the least advantaged and the offices to which the larger rewards are attached are open to all under terms of fair equality of opportunity. No one loses by permitting such inequalities. Hence, the choice of Rawls' two principles.

The hypothetical choice-point from which individuals choose principles is called by Rawls *the original position*. It corresponds to the state of nature of traditional social contract theory. What distinguishes Rawls' original position from more traditional notions of the state of nature is that, when occupying it, people choose their principles from behind what Rawls calls a *veil of ignorance*. That is, they choose without knowing specific items of information about themselves such as what their natural talents are, or to what social class they belong.

We must now turn from exegesis to criticism. How convincing are the considerations which Rawls adduces on behalf of his principles? In particular, how convincing are the arguments which are advanced by Rawls to show that his second principle both accords with our considered moral judgements and would be selected from the original position? It has to be said that his arguments are anything but compelling in their force.

It is true that no has done anything to deserve the natural talents with which they are born or the social class of their parents. *Pace* Rawls, it does not follow that all differences in life-prospects issuing from such non-deserved differences between individuals are *arbitrary* from a moral point of view. As David Gauthier was among the first to point out,[14] Rawls conceives of society as a cooperative venture entered into by individuals for the sake of their mutual advantage. It follows that, for his theory to work, there must be a base-line of non-cooperation against which individuals can measure the advantages of cooperation. This base-line must be how well they each would fare were they not to cooperate.

Each may fare incomparably better by cooperating with others than by not cooperating. Nonetheless, in the absence of cooperation with one another, people may be expected to fare very differently, as a result of differences in their natural endowment. This includes, one might add, differences in the assets put at their disposal by their parents. Now, Rawls himself states that the purpose for which individuals cooperate in society is mutual advantage. It seems overwhelmingly likely that, as a result of being born with superior natural attributes (or with more devoted or better-endowed parents), some individuals, in the absence of cooperating with others who are less well-endowed than themselves, would enjoy superior life-prospects to these others. It must follow that, in such circumstances, it would not be at all arbitrary, on the basis of differences in attributes that no one has done anything to deserve, for the better endowed to enjoy superior life-prospects to those enjoyed by the less well-endowed. For suppose the better endowed would enjoy better life-prospects than the less well-endowed were neither to cooperate with one another. And, suppose, further, that cooperation between the better and less well-endowed is for *mutual* advantage. It follows that, unless the principles of justice governing social cooperation allowed for unequal yet undeserved life-prospects among members, the better-endowed could end up without benefiting from – and hence would be without reason for – cooperating with the less well-endowed. Consequently, contrary to Rawls, it is not at variance with any of our considered moral judgements that those with different natural endowments should, on the basis of these undoubtedly undeserved differences, enjoy different life-prospects from another.

Rawls' intuition to the contrary appears to be based upon his supposing that, if a person does not *deserve* to enjoy better life-prospects than others, then that person deserves *not* to enjoy better life-prospects than these others. This inference seems clearly invalid. Compare: from the fact that a person does not believe that London is the capital of England, it cannot be inferred that the person believes London is not the capital of England. The person may never have heard of either London or England, or if he has have no opinion on the subject. Likewise, a person might not deserve to have been born with the superior life-prospects to others arising from the undeserved better looks or brains with which they have been born. From the fact the person does not, it cannot be inferred that the person deserves not to have been born with superior life-prospects to others arising from these better looks or brains. It certainly cannot be inferred that the person deserves to be denied any better life-prospects than others arising from these attributes on the basis of their having been undeserved. Rawls is undoubtedly correct that those born with superior capacities, or else who acquire them by receiving a better education than others, have done nothing to deserve the greater benefits these superior capacities bring. But neither have these more fortunate people done anything to deserve not enjoying the superior benefits that their superior capacities would bring. The question of the deservingness or otherwise of unequal life-prospects is immaterial to the justice of inequalities of life-prospects arising from differences in natural endowment or other accidents of fortune.

Consequently, contrary to Rawls, it is not at variance with any of our considered moral judgements that, in a system of natural liberty, those with better natural endowments should, on the basis of these undeserved better endowments, enjoy better life-prospects than those less favourably endowed.

Grant that different people have different natural endowments, and that these would supply them with different life-prospects in a pre-social setting. It must also follow that the argument that Rawls offers for the second of his two claims on behalf of his second principle is similarly flawed. Rawls claims that, in order for the choice of principles to be fair and unbiased, those who choose must abstract from a knowledge of what their natural endowments are. Rawls infers that what they would choose would be principles which did not favour those with superior natural endowments to others. However, the contracting parties are expected to know that people *do* have different natural endowments from one another. And, they are entitled to know also that these different natural endowments of people would give their possessors different life-prospects outside the framework of society. Given that the contracting parties know this, why should anyone agree to the difference principle? For, in effect, this principle negates the differences in pre-social life-prospects due to differences in natural endowment. Anyone making any such agreement runs the risk of ending up in society with less than they would outside it. This would hardly be fair.

In order that every contracting party benefit from the entering into society, each should be allowed an equivalent in primary goods to that which they can be expected to obtain for themselves outside society. This will be unequal as a result of differences in natural endowment. From the entire stock of social goods produced in society, an equivalent of each person's entitlement based on natural endowment should be deducted and distributed to each individual. It is only the remaining stock of primary goods which is the specific product of social cooperation that is a fitting subject for distribution equally to all members of society, unless an unequal distribution is to the advantage of even the least well-off. However, such a distribution of the social surplus is precisely what is effected by the system of natural liberty as conceived by Adam Smith and other classical liberals. For within it, the social surplus is created through a set of voluntary agreements which collectively distribute to the several contracting parties the product of their cooperating with one another on a basis which reflects their respective contributions to it. Consequently, Rawls has failed to show that the inequalities that would naturally arise within the system of natural liberty are unjust. In terms of our own formulation of the claims of classical liberalism, Rawls has failed to show that a liberal form of societal order does not enable the life-prospects of all its members to be as good as they legitimately can be.

In reply to this line of objection to his theory, Rawls has denied that it is possible to make any meaningful distinction between what is acquired by individuals as members of society and what would have been acquired by them in a state of nature. He writes, 'since membership in our society is given, . . . we cannot know what we would have been like had we not belonged to it (perhaps the thought lacks sense). . . . Apart from our place and history in society, even our potential abilities cannot be known and our interests and character are still to be formed.'[15]

Because we are creatures whose identity and nature is so much a social artefact, argues Rawls, we can form no determinate notion of what we might or would have been able to obtain for ourselves outside of society, since *we* would not have existed outside society. Thus, Rawls responds, 'no sense can be made of the notion of that part of an individual's social benefits that exceed what would have been their situation in . . . a state of nature'.[16]

To this reply by Rawls, Gauthier has offered the following rejoinder. When it comes to the question of what their different respective capacities should be considered as entitling them to, the fact that human beings are social products is irrelevant. Gauthier writes

> Let us grant that human beings are social products. Do we thereby grant that society, or any group of persons however constituted, acquires any right to these products? That each individual's capacities are actualised within a social nexus does not make them collective rather than individual assets, or afford any ground for treating them as part of the common capital of the group within which the individual is formed. . . . We grant, at least for the purposes of argument that the genesis of individual identity is social. We do not grant that this genesis affects the status of the identity. To be a self one need not be self-made. And each person's

concern with himself, his nature as a maximizer of individual utility, need not be affected by his awareness that social forces have shaped both that concern, and the determinate preferences that provide its content. . . . Impartiality is not achieved by treating persons as if they lacked particular capacities and concerns; indeed impartiality among real persons is violated by such treatment. In supposing that the just distribution of benefits and costs in social interaction is not to be related to the characteristics of the particular individuals who make up society, Rawls violates the integrity of human beings as they are and as they conceive themselves. In seeking to treat persons as pure beings freed from the arbitrariness of their individuating characteristics, Rawls succeeds in treating persons only as social instruments.[17]

Rawls has failed to supply any good reason to deny the moral legitimacy of a form of societal order, such as the liberal polity, which permits its individual members to treat their non-deserved – albeit not undeserved – endowments and capacities as their own, and to enjoy better life-prospects on the basis of them. Accordingly, our final verdict on Rawls must be that he has failed to provide any reason for preferring a modern to a classical liberal form of order.

3.3 IMPARTIALITY, INEQUALITIES OF SACRIFICE, AND LEGITIMACY

A more recent attempt to indict the liberal order for the inequalities permitted within it has been made by Thomas Nagel.[18] Nagel argues against such a form of order even when it incorporates a guaranteed minimum. What is said morally to force upon us a still more egalitarian order is our being able to view the world in two different ways. As well as being able to view the world from a personal standpoint (that is, in terms of how things affect each of us personally), we are each able to view the world from what he calls *an impersonal standpoint.* When so viewed, claims Nagel, we consider the world without reference to which particular person we happen to be within it. When so viewing the world, we cannot but be impartial between ourselves and others. From this standpoint, we must attach equal importance to the lives of everyone, ourselves included. It is only from the personal standpoint that our own interests can assume greater importance to us than the comparable interests of others. Since both the personal and impersonal standpoints are inescapable, the central – and, in Nagel's view, still unsolved – problem of political philosophy is to formulate an acceptable social ideal. This is one that specifies a set of social institutions that simultaneously satisfies both standpoints.

Even were a liberal-capitalist order to incorporate a guaranteed minimum, Nagel argues, it would still fail to be morally acceptable. It would still lack what he calls *legitimacy*. What he means by legitimacy and illegitimacy is explained as follows.

> If a system is legitimate, those living under it have no grounds for complaint against the way its basic structure accommodates their point of view, and no one is morally justified in withholding his cooperation from the functioning of the system, trying to subvert its results, or trying to overturn it if he has the power to do so.
>
> An illegitimate system, on the other hand, treats some of those living under it in such a way that they can reasonably feel that their interests and point of view have not been adequately accommodated – so that, even taking into account the interests of others, their own point of view puts them reasonably in opposition to the system.[19]

Nagel describes in the following general terms the circumstances in which it is reasonable for someone to complain that the social structure of their society has not adequately accommodated their interests. He writes

> What makes it reasonable for someone to reject a system, and therefore makes it illegitimate, is either that it leaves him too badly off by comparison with others . . . , or that it demands too much of him by way of sacrifice of his interests or commitments by comparison with some feasible alternative. . . . [W]hat counts as too badly off or too demanding depends on the cost to others, in these same terms, of the alternative.[20]

Even when it incorporates a guaranteed minimum for everyone, a capitalist society is claimed by Nagel to lack legitimacy. The less well-off are said to have legitimate grounds for complaint against such a form of society. Their grounds, claims Nagel, are that its basic structure demands of them too great a sacrifice of their interests by comparison with a feasible alternative. There is, he says, a feasible alternative which would not require of anyone such large sacrifices of interest. This alternative is provided by a form of order in which there is equality of resources, apart from differences created by individual effort. To institute such a form of order would involve a transfer of resources from the well-off in capitalism to the badly-off in capitalism. However, argues Nagel, it would be unreasonable for the well-off in capitalism to complain about having to make such sacrifices of interest were resources transferred from them to the less well-off so as to establish equality. In terms of the sacrifice it requires of their interests, equality demands less by way of sacrifice of the interests of the well-off than capitalism requires of those of its less well-off. Nagel writes

> It is simply false that the worse off cannot reasonably reject the guaranteed minimum in favour of the standard . . . [of equality]. If they were to accept it, forgoing a more egalitarian system, they would be forgoing benefits above the minimum for themselves, merely in order to avoid depriving the better off of the benefits *they* can enjoy only under the guaranteed minimum, and which they would not enjoy under a more equal system. . . . It is not reasonable for the better off to reject systems significantly more equal than the guaranteed minimum, on the ground that the sacrifice demanded of them by such systems is excessive. Such a standard does not ask enough of our impartiality, as applied to the choice of a social ideal.[21]

Nagel's claim is that an equalizing transfer of resources from the well-off to the less well-off involves the former having to make a lesser sacrifice of their interests than does the non-transfer of these resources involve the less well-off having to make. Impartiality should lead to a universal preference for whichever system involves smaller sacrifices of interest having to be made. Nagel bases this latter claim on two others. The first is an appeal to the diminishing marginal utility of resources, the fact that the more a person has of any good the less each successive unit of that good is worth to one. The second is that an attitude of impartiality between two people will lead to priority being attached to the more urgent needs of one over the less urgent needs and desires of another. Nagel writes

> Transferable resources will usually benefit a person with less more than they will benefit a person with significantly more. So if everyone's benefit counts the same from the . . . [impartial] standpoint, and if there is a presumption in favour of greater benefit, there will be a reason to prefer a more equal to a less equal distribution of a given quantity of resources. [I]mpartiality is also . . . egalitarian in itself . . . mean[ing] that impartiality generates a greater interest in benefiting the worse off than in benefiting the better off – a kind of priority to the former over the latter. The claims on our impartial concern of an individual who is badly off present themselves as having some priority over the claims of each individual who is better off: as being ahead in the queue, so to speak.[22]

Given a choice between an inegalitarian capitalist order or some egalitarian alternative, the moral requiredness of impartiality dictates that egalitarianism is to be preferred on the grounds that it involves lesser sacrifices to be made. What ultimately Nagel claims morally offensive about the liberal form of society, therefore, is that the inequality to be found within it requires a greater sacrifice of interest on the part of the less well-off than would be required of its better-off were a regime of strict equality introduced. It is this conviction which lies behind the following representative statements of Nagel.

> [T]he vast inequalities of wealth and power which even the more egalitarian versions of such systems continue to generate are really incompatible with an adequate response to the impartial attitude which is the first manifestation of the impersonal standpoint. The liberal state may be better than the competition, but it is not good enough.[23]

> [I]f everyone matters just as much as everyone else, it is appalling that the most effective social systems we have been able to devise permit so many people to be born into conditions of harsh deprivation which crush their prospects for leading a decent life, while many others are well provided for from birth, come to control substantial resources, and are free to enjoy advantages vastly beyond the conditions of mere decency.[24]

How compelling is this objection of Nagel's to the liberal form of organization of society? I shall now argue that it rests upon an assumption that is highly questionable to say the least. This assumption is that the less well-off in such a society can be considered to be *sacrificing* greater benefits than they would be able to enjoy in some more egalitarian order. Nagel is, of course, correct in supposing that the less well-off may gain some short-term temporary benefit from a radical redistribution of assets from the better-off to them. However, whether such a redistribution would be to their net advantage – and, hence, whether failure to effect it involves some sacrifice of their interests – depends upon whether the overall long-term interests of the less well-off in capitalism *would* be served better by such egalitarian redistribution. It is not obvious that they would. Suppose it were to become forbidden for people to accumulate more assets than were attributable to their individual personal effort. It would follow that no one would have any incentive to accumulate beyond what they could personally consume within their lifetime: bequest would be impermissible. There would be great incentive for capital consumption rather than capital formation which depends upon saving. In a regime which accords with Nagel's strong egalitarian social ideals, the disincentives for capital formation arising from the prohibition of unearned inequality might well be so great as ultimately to leave its members worse-off than those who are least well-off within a liberal order which permits unequal concentrations of wealth to accumulate. In the absence of having demonstrated why this should not occur were a liberal order to become egalitarian through massive transfer of assets, Nagel's argument fails to demonstrate that the less well-off in a liberal order have grounds for legitimate complaint in terms of sacrifices of interest they are being obliged to forgo.

Moreover, were this form of order to be as illegitimate as Nagel claims it to be, then presumably it should never have been permitted to come into existence in the first place. However, had it not done so, it is unlikely that the wealth that the better-off enjoy within it would have been brought into existence in the first place. Had it not been, then the less well-off can hardly claim to be making a sacrifice in not having an equal share of it. For had they *been* eligible for an equal share of it, it would never have existed! How can a system be judged illegitimate on the grounds of *depriving* some members of benefits that simply would not have existed under a more legitimate system?

Nagel might reply that an egalitarian redistribution of unequal resources would not so discourage capital formation and investment as to prevent the redistribution being to the net disadvantage of those who would be its immediate beneficiaries. Such a reply lacks credibility. A form of egalitarianism of the sort advocated by Nagel must prohibit individuals from being able to accumulate assets they are capable of bequeathing to those whom they choose. It is highly doubtful whether such a prohibition could in the long run serve anyone's interests. Accordingly, we may reject Nagel's objection to the legitimacy of the liberal order. He has failed to show it rests upon any genuine sacrifices of interest on the part of the less well-off within it.

3.4 EQUAL WORTH, EQUAL TREATMENT AND EQUALITY OF RESOURCES

In an influential series of papers,[25] Ronald Dworkin has argued that the inequalities which are permitted within it suffice to render morally illegitimate that form of order advocated by classical liberals. According to Dworkin, such inequalities are capable of being tolerated by a government only when it fails to treat all its citizens with that degree of equal concern and respect to which they are all entitled as human beings. In order for government to so treat its citizens as equals, it is not enough that they all be accorded equal rights to life, liberty, and property, in the sense of an equal right to acquire and hold property. To treat them as equals, government must accord them a right to equal property, in the sense of a right to an equal share in the resources at the disposal of society. Thus, he writes, '[t]reating people as equals requires that each be permitted to use, for the projects to which he devotes his life, no more than an equal share of the resources available'.[26]

Dworkin is at pains to point out that the equality of resources which equal worth makes mandatory is not the same as an equal share of all wealth. For if people start out with equal resources at their disposal, including time, they might end up with different quantities of wealth, depending upon how they choose to dispose of those resources. However, Dworkin is equally at pains to point out that the equality of resources he considers mandatory requires that no one, over their lifetime, have at their disposal anything other than an equal share of the community's stock of resources, where this stock includes the collective set of individual natural talents and time.

Were everyone to start out life with equal raw skill and amounts of wealth, and were they to enjoy the same degree of fortune over their lives, then a liberal order would be consistent with the enjoyment by everyone of equality of resources. For, in such circumstances, any final unequal distribution of wealth that would arise would be the product of how different people had chosen to dispose of their equal resources according to their individual schedules of preference. However, life is not like that. People differ in natural talent, social class, and luck. The inequalities of wealth that result from these differences, claims Dworkin, are unfair. He writes

> In the real world people do not start their lives on equal terms; some begin with marked advantages of family wealth or of formal and informal education. Others suffer because their race is despised. Luck plays a further and sometimes devastating part in deciding who gains or keeps jobs everyone wants. Quite apart from these plain inequalities, people are not in fact equal in raw skill or intelligence or other native capacities. . . . So some people who are perfectly willing, even anxious, to make exactly the choices about work and consumption and saving that other people make end up with fewer resources, and no plausible theory of equality can accept this as fair.[27]

On Dworkin's view, it is incompatible with the equal treatment which they merit receiving from their government that the latter should tolerate its citizens possessing unequal resources as a result of differences in natural talent, family background, or just luck. Accordingly, it follows, on Dworkin's view, that any form of order such as that advocated by classical liberals, which tolerates such forms of inequality, cannot be morally legitimate.

Market allocations must be corrected in order to bring some people closer to the share of resources they would have had but for these various differences of initial advantage, luck, and inherent capacity.[28]

For government to treat its citizens as equals . . . resources and opportunities should be distributed, so far as possible, equally, so that roughly the same share of whatever is available is directed to satisfying the ambitions of each. Any other general aim of distribution will assume either that the fate of some people should be of greater concern that of others, or that the ambition or talents of some are more worthy, and should be supported more generously on that account.[29]

How compelling are the grounds on which Dworkin bases his indictment of the form of order advocated by classical liberals? The argument would appear to suffer from one fundamental defect. It assumes that, other than within a form of order which, like that advocated by classical liberals, permits individuals to appropriate their own natural talents and whatever else is unowned by anyone else, it would be possible for society to know what it has at its disposal, either by way of natural talent among its populace or by way of natural resources. Should, as classical liberals maintain, this assumption be clearly mistaken, then government would be unable to effect any such form of distribution. Of course, given a liberal form of order, government can *ex post facto* acquire a knowledge of what talent and resources exist.

Dworkin might claim that the requirement that it treat its citizens equally imposes upon government the obligation to redistribute the collective assets that have come to its knowledge so as to correct for differences between individual members in luck, natural talent and social class. Such a claim, however, overlooks the fact that these assets only came into existence under one system of rules which applied equally to all citizens. When a government expropriates and redistributes previously appropriated assets in order to create equality of resources among its citizens, it fails to treat with respect those of its citizens with whom it breaks trust by expropriating these assets. Far from being implied by the principle that government treat its citizens with equal concern and respect, redistributive measures involving coercion designed to establish equality of resources are inconsistent with it.

Dworkin, thus, fails to appreciate the innocuousness and benefit to every member of that form of social order which permits its members to appropriate, hold, and transfer at will, assets which, at the time of the appropriation, are not anyone else's. A similar failure to appreciate that these virtues belong to the liberal order vitiates another recent attempt to argue on behalf of greater equality of resources than is mandatory or likely in a liberal order.

3.5   RADICAL EGALITARIANISM AND THE FORMAL PRINCIPLE OF JUSTICE

Kai Nielsen[30] has recently sought to defend a position he calls *radical egalitarianism* through invoking a principle he calls *the formal principle of justice*. In essence, what Nielsen intends to denote by the former expression is equality of life-prospects. If asked to explain why such a measure of equality should be thought desirable, Nielsen confesses himself to be somewhat at a loss. He writes

> We are, I believe, so close to bedrock here that it is difficult to know what to say. That such a condition is desirable gives expression, to speak autobiographically for a moment, to a root pre-analytical (pre-theoretical) conception of what fairness between persons comes to. . . .
> I have in mind the sense of unfairness which goes with the acceptance, where something non-catastrophic could be done about it, of the existence of very different life prospects of equally talented, equally energetic children from very different social backgrounds: say the children of a successful businessman and a dishwasher. Their whole life prospects are very unequal indeed and, given the manifest quality of that difference, that this should be so seems to me very unfair. It conflicts sharply with my sense of justice.[31]

While interesting as a piece of autobiographical information, such a disclosure hardly amounts to an argument for radical egalitarianism. To his credit, Nielsen recognizes this to be the case. He does attempt to supply an argument in support of the deliverance of his sense of justice. It appeals to a principle which Nielsen calls, as do many others, *the formal principle of justice*. This principle states that we must treat like cases alike. Nielsen claims to find in this principle a basis of support for his radically egalitarian moral intuitions by arguing as follows.

> We all, if we are not utterly zany, want a life in which our needs are satisfied and in which we can live as we wish and do what we want to do. Though we differ in many ways, in our abilities, capacities for pleasure, determination to keep on with a job, we do not differ about wanting our needs satisfied or being able to live as we wish. Thus, *ceteris paribus*, where questions of desert, entitlement, and the like do

not enter, it is only fair that all of us should have our needs equally considered and that we should, again *ceteris paribus*, all be able to do as we wish in a way compatible with others doing likewise. From the formal principle of justice and a few key facts about us, we can get to the claim that *ceteris paribus*, we should go for this much equality. But this is the core content of radical egalitarianism.[32]

This is supposedly an argument on behalf of an ideal whose aim is that society 'provide the social basis for equality of life prospects such that there cannot be anything like the vast disparities in whole life prospects that exist now'.[33] Judged by reference to the social ideal which Nielsen seeks to recommend, the argument must be judged less than compelling. The formal principle of justice that we must treat like cases alike cannot provide support for radical egalitarianism, even when conjoined with the fact that we are all alike in having needs and wants that we would like satisfied. All that may be inferred from the conjunction of the principle and this similarity between us, is that, *ceteris paribus* (all other things being equal between us), we should all be given the wherewithal for the equal satisfaction of our respective wants and needs. However, it is anything but the case that, apart from our different wants and needs, all else is equal between us. For a start, there are our different natural talents. Then there is our different degrees of willingness to use our talents, the difference in talents and natural endowment of our different loved ones, and so on and so on. More than this, apart from our all having wants and needs that we would like satisfied, there is another important respect in which most, if not all of us, are similar to each other. We are alike in willing to exert an effort only under the stimulus of self-interest or confined generosity. Given differences of natural talent, this other similarity implies that a system of incentives will be needed to bring forth effort that is bound to lead to inequality of outcome.

3.6 WELL-BEING, EQUALITY AND THE POLITICS OF THE LEFT

Ted Honderich is among the latest in a line of philosophers on the left who have attempted to demonstrate that the form of societal order advocated by classical liberals serves society's less-advantaged members less well than does a more egalitarian and redistributive one. His argument is set out in a recent critical study of the entire tradition – or, more accurately, set of traditions – of political thought on the right to which classical liberalism belongs.[34] To this tradition, or set of traditions, Honderich somewhat misleadingly gives the name, 'Conservatism'. Its principal distinguishing characteristic – or, as Honderich prefers to call it, distinction – is its commitment to the institution of private property, to extending it into as wide a domain as possible, and to an attendant market economy.

Honderich examines the rationale for the commitment to private property offered by those who share it. He concludes that there is none, besides a selfish concern on their part to cling on to positions of power and privilege created and safeguarded by the form of order they recommend. By contrast, so he argues, what underlies and provides the rationale of the political commitment of the left is a genuine moral principle. This principle he calls, *the Principle of Equality*. It runs as follows.

> The goal or end of a society must be to make well-off those who are badly-off, by the policy of increasing the means to well-being and of transferring unused means from the well-off, the policy of transferring means which will affect their well-being, and the policy of reducing inequalities having to do with incentive or compensation, these three policies to be advanced in good part by practices of equality.[35]

Practices of equality, we are told, include democracy and the equal provision of many goods and many opportunities, taking into account the fact that unequal need justifies unequal goods.

Underlying Honderich's Principle is a certain conception of human well-being. Honderich equates this condition with the satisfaction of a set of fundamental desires or wants the possession of which he takes to be definitive of human nature. He writes

> All of us share in certain fundamental desires: for the material means to a decent length of life, for ourselves and those close to us; for further material goods, say those supplied by dentists rather than interior decorators, which make life easier; for kinds of freedom and control of our lives in our societies and in smaller contexts, such as work; for the respect of others and also self-respect; for kinds of intimate and other relations with others; for various goods of culture, including knowledge and skill.[36]

The badly-off are said to be those who lack satisfaction of or who are only minimally satisfied in respect of any of these desires.

The Principle of Equality itself incorporates two distinct conceptions. The first is a conception of the proper end or goal of society, namely, its bringing about the well-being of its members. The second is a conception of the best means for achieving this end, namely, its adoption of the practices and policies recommended by the principle rather than those advocated by classical liberals.

There is little in the first of these conceptions to which a classical liberal need take exception. Some classical liberals have preferred not to speak of society as having a goal or end as such. They have preferred instead to conceive of society as an association designed to further the different individual ends of its individual members. On the other hand, given that, among the desires whose satisfaction is said to be necessary for well-being are those for freedom and self-determination, the overall goal or end for society that Honderich lays down is one that can be accepted without embarrassment by classical liberals.

Matters are very much otherwise as regards the second of his two conceptions, namely, his conception of the best means for attaining his favoured end. Honderich is acutely aware of the various arguments which classical liberals give for considering the egalitarian order preferred by Honderich to be less able than their own preferred market order to advance the well-being of members of a society. He claims that none of these arguments is convincing. To decide whether he is correct, we must examine Honderich's reasons for rejecting these arguments.

As we earlier did ourselves, Honderich classifies the arguments of classical liberals for their preferred form of order into two main sorts, economic and non-economic. The economic arguments seek to establish that the principal institutions of a liberal order – namely, private property, a market economy and minimal government – are better able than the more egalitarian social institutions and practices advocated by the Principle of Equality to satisfy the desires of members of society for material goods. The non-economic arguments are designed to show the former set of institutions to be better able than the latter to satisfy the several other desires whose satisfaction is necessary for well-being, such as that for freedom.

Honderich divides the economic arguments into two. He calls them the *Incentive Argument* and the *Hidden Hand Vindication*. The Incentive Argument appeals to certain alleged facts about human psychology. These facts are supposed to show that the economic rewards for productive effort provided by a market economy offer more effective incentives for such effort than does reliance upon other forms of motivation, such as altruism. The alleged characteristics of human psychology cited in support of this thesis are its confined generosity and predominant self-centredness.

Honderich finds himself unmoved by the Incentive Argument. He argues that the conception of human nature upon which it rests is overly narrow. It fails to recognize other possible sources of motivation besides the prospect of monetary reward as potential incentives for contributing to society's economic well-being. Among the other possible sources of motivation, according to Honderich, are social altruism, the anticipated satisfaction of achievement, distinction and increased power, and, finally, the threat of punishment or other penalty for failing to contribute.

How compelling is this objection of Honderich's to the Incentive Argument? In the opinion of the present author, not very. Honderich's proposed alternatives to reliance on market incentives are not promising. The primary consideration that serves to persuade classical liberals of the superior efficacy of the market system, rather than reliance upon any other system of incentives, is not a belief in the confined generosity of human beings. Rather, it is a recognition of the limits of human knowledge about how the well-being of members of a society can best be served by any member, plus a belief that the price system in a free market is the best form of communications system there is for transmitting such information to economic agents. As Hayek has observed,

> All the possible differences in men's moral attitudes amount to little so far as their significance for social organization is concerned, compared with the fact that all man's mind can effectively comprehend are the facts of the narrow circle of which he is the centre; that, whether he is completely selfish or the most perfect altruist, the human needs for which he can effectively care are an almost negligible fraction of the needs of all members of society. The real question therefore is not whether man is, or ought to be, guided by selfish motives but whether we can allow him to be guided in his actions by those immediate consequences which he can know and care for or whether he ought to be made to do what seems appropriate to somebody else who is supposed to possess a fuller comprehension of the significance of these actions to society as whole.[37]

Apart from this consideration, however, there are very good reasons for rejecting Honderich's suggestion that compulsion be used as an incentive rather than economic reward. Honderich rhetorically asks

> Why should members of a society not be compelled, constrained, led, called upon, encouraged, argued into . . . , convinced, educated, re-educated or inspired to contribute to its economic well-being somehow conceived? . . . Why should we proceed differently here than with the good end of securing obedience to the criminal law?[38]

There are several good reasons why society should not seek to use the sanctions of the law to compel socially beneficial conduct, rather than mere harm-avoidance, as classical liberals advocate. At least four considerations might be offered against the suggestion. First, while it is reasonably clear to everyone what sorts of act on the part of someone result in others being harmed, the same cannot be said about what sorts of action constitute failing to benefit another. Accordingly, it is relatively easy to frame a legal and moral prohibition against anyone harming anyone else that can be both easily acted on by everyone, as well as enforced by the legal and judicial system and by the pressure of moral opinion. By contrast, there is simply no way of anyone knowing nearly as easily, with respect to any particular act he or she might be contemplating performing, whether or not it is an instance of failing to benefit another. Even rescuing a drowning man by throwing him a rope cannot easily be known not to be an instance of failing to benefit another. For even though failing to save the drowning man can be said to be an instance of failing to save and therefore benefit him, it does not follow that saving and thereby benefiting him is not also simultaneously an instance of failing to benefit someone else.

Any judicial and moral system that sought to compel altruistic acts in the way Honderich suggests to be possible and desirable would have to spell out a series of detailed prescriptions of what individuals had both to do and to refrain from doing, in different sorts of circumstance, in order to avoid failing to benefit others and thereby liability to incur the imposition of negative sanctions. It is inconceivable that any such code could be produced that would not immediately reveal itself to be hopelessly ineffective in achieving its objective. A system of law can clearly stipulate what people must do and refrain from doing in order to avoid harming others. But how can legislation stipulate clearly what individuals must do and also refrain from doing in order to avoid being deemed to have failed to benefit others?

The second reason against compelling beneficence by law is this. If legal and moral censure is to be applied to people for failing to benefit others, what sanctions are to be used for discouraging people from positively harming others? And, for what are people to be rewarded and praised, in a society in which it is necessary to avoid failing to benefit others in order to escape moral censure and legal punishment?

Third, as Franz Brentano has pointed out, the making of beneficence legally and morally obligatory would have highly detrimental consequences. He observes

> Duties of love are often neglected and infringed upon in a most inflammatory manner, particularly during eras in which the spirit of mankind has alienated itself from religious ideals and is intent only upon gain and pleasure. At such times loud voices are to be heard urging . . . [that]

the mere existence of duties of love, unsupported by any power to enforce them, is not enough, and consequently . . . work[ing] to make them compulsory. They regard force as more effective than love and goodness against self-seeking and the greed for profit.[39]

Such a proposal, says Brentano, 'contains grounds for grave misgivings'.[40] He writes

When freedom is withdrawn, the most noble delights and virtues find no nourishment and wither. What place is there for the bliss of doing good or the fulfilment of the duties of love if everything is done under compulsion? In such a society, fear becomes the motive for doing good, but fear is torment; in an order based upon freedom of ownership it is hope, and hope is joy.[41]

Henry Sidgwick has offered a fourth reason why it is better for people to be motivated to perform acts beneficial to others by means of such external incentives as the market supplies rather than by appeals to social pressure and social altruism. He observes that, except in cases of unforeseen sudden calamity that render someone unable to provide for themselves, the general happiness is promoted by far the most effectively through 'maintaining in adults generally (except married women) the expectation that each will be thrown on his own resources for the supply of his own wants'.[42] Such an expectation would be undermined by a legal system which compelled people to benefit others, as well as simply to avoid harming them.

There are, then, surely, very good reasons for rejecting Honderich's proposal that beneficence be created by means of social compulsion rather than by an appeal to the self-interest of agents through market incentives.

The Hidden Hand Vindication of market institutions and private property comprises a bundle of propositions drawn from the discipline of economics. These propositions all variously purport to show that 'if each of us seeks selfishly our own personal profit, this may somehow and mysteriously serve a general end, the good as it is somehow conceived of society as a whole'.[43] Six such propositions are identified and considered by Honderich. These are as follows. First, the system of external incentives which is part of a capitalist economy motivates agents to work harder and be more creative and entrepreneurial than they otherwise would. Second, a market economy 'brings to bear a greater knowledge on every aspect of the devising, manufacturing and distributing of goods'.[44] Third, 'a larger private sector involves less of the waste which results from producing what no one wants'.[45] Fourth, a private property capitalist economy best conserves natural resources. Fifth, a capitalist system minimizes the costs of administration and decision-making. Sixth, a capitalist economy is more efficient than any other in distributing resources.

Against the Hidden Hand Vindication, Honderich appeals, in the first instance, to the general disputability of all such propositions as these emanating from so eminently contentious a discipline as economics. To illustrate their disputability, Honderich makes two observations. The first is that technological progress has not been confined to capitalist societies. The second is that waste, depletion of natural resources, and industrial pollution have not been confined to non-capitalist ones.

This consideration in itself, however, is hardly conclusive. The constituent propositions of the Vindication may be said to be disputable in one of two ways. First, they may be said to be disputable in the sense of being such that people can, and as a matter of fact have, taken exception to each and every one. This is true of the propositions, but is hardly to the point. It can be observed of each and every one of these propositions that, in this same sense, their contradictories have been advanced in economics and, there, have equally had exception taken to them. Since for every pair of mutually contradictory propositions, one or other must be true, yet both are equally disputable in the sense currently under discussion, it follows that being disputable in this sense is no reason in itself for supposing any one of them to be false.

There is only one credible sense in which the disputability of the propositions of the Vindication can be offered as grounds for withholding assent to them. This is that sense of the expression in which it means 'worthy of being disputed'. However, the disputability of the propositions in the first sense is no grounds for believing in their disputability in this second sense. In order to provide convincing reasons for supposing these propositions disputable in the sense of being worthy of being disputed more is required than mere assertion of their disputability in this sense. It is necessary for there to be supplied a *reason* for supposing them disputable in this second sense. The fact they are disputable in the first sense does not constitute such grounds. Yet it is their disputability in this first sense upon which Honderich primarily relies in seeking to undermine their credentials.

As remarked, Honderich does offer some considerations to illustrate the disputability of the propositions in this second sense. Yet none is at all persuasive. First, Honderich asserts that great technological progress has been made in non-capitalist societies 'including our own societies at certain moments'.[46] One wonders precisely what he has in mind. Can it be doubted that, as matter of historical fact, there has been nothing like the volume of sustained technological development directly designed to be of benefit to the masses as there has been in capitalism? Second, Honderich observes that great waste results from, or consists in, the great concentrations of property that can be and are amassed in capitalist societies by means of its private property system. Again, one wonders precisely what Honderich has in mind here. Is it that the rich expend resources on luxuries for themselves which could otherwise have been deployed to better effect catering for the more urgent needs of the less well-off? If so, then such allegedly self-indulgent use of these resources counts as waste only if one or other of the following two alternatives is genuinely possible. The first is that these same resources might have been brought into existence and yet deployed on behalf of the badly-off, rather than on behalf of the well-off, even in the absence of the private property market system which made it possible for the well-off to bring into being these resources and deploy them for their own advantage rather than for that of the badly-off. The second alternative is that these same resources might have been brought into existence and yet deployed on behalf of the badly-off, rather than the well-off, despite the existence of the private property system which, as matter of fact, made it possible for the well-off to deploy these resources on their own behalf rather than on behalf of the badly-off.

Nothing Honderich says provides reason for thinking either of these two alternative counter-factuals is a genuine possibility. For either to be so, it would have also to be true, of whoever, in the counter-factual situation, brought these resources into being or made them serviceable for human use, that they were moved by motives other than those which moved those who actually brought into being the resources deemed waste by Honderich. They would have to have been moved either by a much greater degree of what Honderich calls 'social altruism' or else by fear of the application of legal and moral sanctions backing laws and mores forbidding the pursuit of self-interest in the manner in which it was as matter of historical fact pursued by the actual producers of these resources. To pursue this matter further would take us into the domain of the Incentive Argument which we have defended against Honderich's criticisms of it. It seems next to inpossible to imagine that human beings could, or even should, have had the psychologies or legal and moral systems they would have needed in order to have been capable of being moved by either of these two sets of motives in a way that led them to be as economically beneficial to all as capitalism enables them to be.

Honderich cites as a third reason for rejecting the Hidden Hand Vindication the depletion by private corporations of natural resources such as rainforests. For such activity to establish Honderich's point, however, what he would need to establish is that such corporations would have been both able and had the economic incentives to wreak such havoc upon the rain-forests in the sorts of political order favoured by classical liberals. It is doubtful if he could establish this. Indeed, the opposite seems true. Such destruction of natural assets is liable to occur only when governments deliberately distort market forces in ways that are opposed by classical liberals. As has been observed in connection with the destruction of the Amazon rainforests,

> In Brazil, the government has expanded cattle ranching in the Amazon by offering subsidies and tax incentives. . . . Agricultural settlement, which has also been promoted by government investments in land settlement programs and by road building, has been the second most important cause of tropical forest destruction in Brazil. Other govern-ment investments have brought even more destruction. The Tucurui hydro-electric project on the Tocanto river, for example, was built at a cost of about $4 billion and has flooded 2,160 square kilometres of forest land.[47]

If governments were limited in the way proponents of the Hidden Hand advocate, these problems that concern Honderich here would not arise.

We turn now to a consideration of the objections which Honderich offers to the various non-economic arguments for capitalism which he considers. Like their economic counterparts, the non-economic argu-ments seek to establish that private property, market institutions, and lim-ited government are necessary for the well-being of members of society. Unlike the economic arguments, the non-economic ones seek to do so by claiming these institutions to be necessary conditions of certain non-material goods such as freedom. The principal goods for which such claims have been made and on which Honderich focuses are the follow-ing: the natural (or moral) right to property, social stability, the family, civilization, and freedom of various sorts. Honderich disputes the validity of each of these claims. Either he denies market institutions and limited government to be necessary conditions of these goods, or else he denies these goods to be essential for well-being.

The appeal to natural rights as a defence of property is dismissed as begging the question. On Honderich's view, 'to say someone has some sort of non-legal right to something is just to say, with some relatively unimportant preamble, addition or implication, that he *ought to have the thing if he so chooses*'.[48] It thus follows, claims Honderich, that to say that society ought to acknowledge private property because individuals have moral rights to it, 'is at bottom to say that society ought to be that way because that is the way it ought to be'.[49] Appeal to a natural right to property does not provide any independent defence of the institution.

The force of Honderich's dismissal of appeal to a moral (or natural) right to property depends on his being right about rights. His analysis of what having a natural right amounts to is somewhat under-argued and offers a somewhat perfunctory treatment of what is a very complex and difficult subject. First of all, contrary to what he asserts, we are ordinarily far from thinking that someone has a right to whatever he ought to have if he so chooses. To take a now-famous example offered by Judith Jarvis Thomson.[50] Suppose a child has been given a box of chocolates by a relative and refuses to give any to a younger sibling who has asked for one. Although we might be of the opinion that the deprived sibling ought to be given a chocolate if he chooses, few of us might hold that the sibling denied a chocolate had a right to any of them.

Let us then set Honderich's analysis of rights on one side and turn to a more nuanced account such as that of John Stuart Mill. If we do, then Honderich's objection to the appeal to a supposed moral right to private property loses its force. Mill defined a right in the following manner. 'To have a right . . . is to have something which society ought to defend me in the possession of.'[51] Honderich might well be prepared to accept Mill's analysis of a right but deny it casts any doubt on his general point. Honderich might simply ask for a reason *why* society ought to defend people in the possession of private property. But Mill does provide the beginnings of a good explanation why society ought to defend people in the possession of private property. Mill's view was that what society ought to defend people in the possession of were those things that were most essential to their happiness. It turns out on this view that life and personal liberty qualify for being things to which human beings may be said to have a moral right. But arguably so is private property, and precisely this was what was argued by the classical economists. In order for Honderich to show that classical liberals are wrong to maintain there is a moral right to private property, what he needs to provide is some reason for doubting that the institution of private property is essential to the happiness of everyone. He has so far conspicuously failed to offer any such reason.

Against the claim that extensive private property is a necessary condition of political stability, Honderich offers the blunt denial that the institution is either a necessary or sufficient condition of such a putative *desideratum*. In any case, he observes, since not all political stability is worth having, the conduciveness of the institution to political stability is not in itself a recommendation for it.

A propos Honderich's denial that a system of extensive private property is a necessary condition of enduring political stability, and his assertion that not all stability is good, two observations are in order. First, while it is true that some societies have enjoyed enduring political stability in the absence of extensive private property and a market economy, it is false that any have enjoyed political stability and economic growth and affluence without these institutions. Second, although some societies which have enjoyed these institutions might have failed to be politically stable, it nonetheless is true that none which has enjoyed these institutions has collapsed through internal rather than external causes. Advocates of capitalism were uniquely wont to point out that, between people who were otherwise divided by religious or ethnic differences, commercial transactions and relations fostered mutual tolerance and civility.[52]

A similar sort of argumentative move as he makes about stability is made by Honderich in relation to the claim that property is a necessary condition of the family. Property is neither a necessary condition of this institution, nor is the institution always a good thing.

Honderich may well be correct in claiming that there can be families in the absence of the institution of private property. However, it is doubtful that families can flourish where the spouses do not possess private property of their own. The thesis that private property is essential to the institution of the family has to be understood as the claim that private property is good for families. Honderich concedes that it might be, but denies this is a recommendation of private property apparently on the grounds that families are not always good for their members. The existence of unhappy families, however, does not establish Honderich's point. Even those who are victims of unhappy families, for example, children of estranged parents or unloved spouses unable to obtain a divorce, might still be net beneficiaries of the existence of the institution of the family. The existence of unhappy families at most establishes only that not everyone is better-off living in the family unit within which they live. Their existence does not establish that not everyone is better-off living in *some* family unit or other of their own. Nor does it establish that everyone is not better-off living in societies in which the family unit is the norm. There is very strong reason for thinking everyone benefits from living in societies in which the family unit is the norm, as well as for thinking that all children benefit from growing up within a family unit, at least to the age of maturity.

The question, then, becomes whether the family unit is a more viable unit within capitalism than in other forms of society. There is very strong reason for thinking this to be so. There is also strong reason for thinking that the family unit is very much undermined, with grave social consequences, when forms of provision are established in society for the maintenance of mothers with small children in their care besides the expectation that it is the prime responsibility of the fathers of those children to provide it.

Honderich rejects the claim that private property is necessary for civilization on the grounds of the vagueness of the claim. Because it is left so vague, he says, it is impossible to tell whether it is true. In advancing the claim that institution of private property is essential for civilization, classical liberals leave the term 'civilization' undefined. But is this a sufficient reason for dismissing the claim, as Honderich claims? I cannot see that this is so. First of all, it is not true that the term is always left undefined. Hayek is among those who have advanced this claim and has stated that what we call 'civilization' is 'social life especially in its more advanced forms'.[53] He equates the advance of civilization with the growth 'through selective elimination of less suitable conduct'[54] of 'all human adaptations to environment in which past experience has been incorporated'.[55] He explicitly equates the advance of civilization with the advances of knowledge, skills, tools and institutions. Classical liberals claim that private property is conducive to civilization on the grounds of its facilitating social experimentation in ways of living, which increases rate of invention and transmission of better ways of doing things. I cannot see any reason for supposing this claim does not merit serious discussion.

Honderich expresses corresponding dissatisfaction with the terminology employed by classical liberals in maintaining private property and market economy to be necessary conditions of freedom. The term 'freedom' is not univocal, he observes. Classical liberals use the expression to mean the absence of constraint or restraint deliberately designed to prevent someone doing something. This negative condition, says Honderich, only constitutes one necessary condition of someone's being able to do that thing. It can equally be said, so he claims, that, unless people have such an ability, they are not free to do that thing, notwithstanding their enjoying the negative condition called freedom by classical liberals. As well as enjoying this negative condition, therefore, before someone may truly be said to be free to do a thing, that person must, in addition, possess all the other positive and negative conditions which are severally necessary and jointly sufficient to render that person able to do that thing. Thus, to be free to shop at Harrods, a person not only needs the absence of deliberately imposed restraints designed to prevent him from shopping there. He also needs other resources. In this case, to be free to shop at Harrods requires the pecuniary means to be able to do so. Without these, he is not free to shop there, despite there being no deliberately imposed constraints designed to prevent him from so doing.

Having disambiguated the expression, 'freedom', Honderich goes on to distinguish several different varieties of it. There are said to be two main types of freedom: political and non-political. Political freedom includes freedom to choose and influence government. People possess it when they possess freedom to vote, to express opinion, and to demonstrate. Non-political freedom is freedom to do other things of which the three most important species are civil, social and economic. Civil freedom consists in such things as equality before the law, freedom from arbitrary arrest, freedom of speech, freedom of information, freedom of the press, and freedom of organization, and religious freedom. Social freedoms are said to include 'freedom from poverty, freedom to develop one's capabilities by way of a university education, freedom from want in old age, and freedom from racial and other discrimination'.[56] Economic freedom is freedom to acquire, hold and transfer property.

Honderich concedes that market institutions, private property and limited government are likely to be highly conducive to economic freedom of at least the able-bodied. But he denies that these institutions are at all conducive to any of the other sorts of freedom. He offers two main reasons for this denial. First, these institutions are not sufficient to prevent society succumbing to totalitarianism. Hence, they are not sufficient to preserving political and civil freedoms. Second, these institutions are positively inimical to many of the other freedoms. This is alleged to be most notably so in the case of the social freedoms. For these, claims Honderich, what are needed are 'welfare rights, social security rights, health and educational rights'.[57] Mention of these latter helps us better understand precisely what measures Honderich has in mind in his principle of equality for securing the well-being of the badly-off.

It must be conceded to Honderich that private property and a market economy might not be sufficient to guarantee the avoidance of totalitarianism and hence the preservation of political and civil freedom. However, they might nonetheless be a far better defence of these freedoms than any other alternative set of institutions. This is because they effectively limit the power of government. Because of this, the greater degree of governmental intervention and activity that would be called for by the political programme recommended by Honderich's Principle of Equality carries with it a great danger of political unfreedom, even in conditions of democracy. As John Gray has rightly observed, '[n]o system of government in which property rights and basic liberties are open to revision by temporary political majorities can be regarded as satisfying liberal requirements'.[58]

As for civil freedoms, such restrictions as classical liberals have wanted to place upon trade unions were not intended to restrict the ability of workers to form trade unions or strike. Laws for secret ballots in cases of strikes, for limited numbers of strike pickets, against secondary picketing, and against the closed shop are only intended to prevent trade unionists from coercing others through intimidation.

As for the social freedoms, the form of capitalism which classical liberals support is one which they believe delivers the maximum of such social freedoms to everyone, even if they are not enshrined as recipient welfare rights. Classical liberals believe that, in practice, these social freedoms can be better secured through the basic economic, political and civil liberties they advocate than through governments enshrining in law such extensive rights to welfare as socialists and welfare-state liberals recommend. These social freedoms are not necessarily better provided through being acknowledged as a universal legal entitlement. This is especially so, if the result of making them such is that the goods to which these rights are supposed to entitle people become of very poor quality or simply non-existent. That, when made a legal entitlement, these goods are likely to be inferior in quality, in insufficient supply, or both, is the chief reservation which classical liberals have to any social freedoms being made a legal entitlement. For much the same sort of reason, it is unclear that a political order is capable of doing away with racial discrimination simply by making it a criminal offence.

The upshot of our examination of Honderich's strictures against these arguments for capitalism which he considers is that none of his objections has any force. This being so, he has failed to demonstrate that a society ordered in accordance with the practices and policies recommended by his Principle of Equality would better promote the well-being of its less well-off than would the form of order advocated by classical liberals.

This almost completes my review of the case of modern liberals against that form of social organization advocated by classical liberalism. To conclude discussion at this juncture, however, would be to fail to give explicit consideration to one very important strand of criticism of it advanced in the name of a greater degree of equality than it is claimed to provide. This strand of criticism is that advanced by contemporary feminists in the name of sexual equality. I shall take up this feminist objections to classical liberalism in the next and concluding section of this chapter.

3.7 THE MODERN FEMINIST CRITIQUE OF CLASSICAL LIBERALISM

In 1861, John Stuart Mill published a tract entitled *The Subjection of Women*. At that time, the form of social order that Mill claimed maximally conducive to women's emancipation was precisely that advocated by classical liberals. With one or two notable and highly anomalous exceptions,[59] however, today, virtually all those who style themselves feminists, or as sympathetic to it, are uniformly hostile to this form of societal order. The hostility of latter-day feminists to the liberal order is grounded upon their conviction that it is inimical to the interests of women. More specifically, latter-day feminist critics of the liberal form of order maintain that the political and civil rights it accords are insufficient to provide women members of society with justice and to spare them from subordination to men. At bottom, modern feminists condemn these rights as inadequate on the grounds that they permit the perpetuation of a form of division of labour between the sexes that has been endemic throughout history, and which, so modern feminists maintain, condemns women to a 'lesser life' than that which it enables men to enjoy.

At the core of the offending sexual division of labour lies a different set of expectations placed upon men and women as regards the children they have. Women are expected to be their primary carers; men their primary providers. By 'primary carer', I mean that adult in whose charge a preschool child is placed for a larger portion of the week than the child is placed with any other adult or number of adults. This set of asymmetrical expectations placed upon men and women in relation to their children is considered by virtually all latter-day feminists, and their sympathizers, to put women at an enormous comparative disadvantage *vis-à-vis* men. It impedes the ability of women upon their having children to engage in full-time paid employment outside the home. This impediment is said to have enormously deleterious consequences for women. It leads them to become economically dependent upon the fathers of their children, as well as to enjoy less economic and political power. In short, the offending sexual division of labour is held to perpetuate a system of male domination and female subordination. Some representative quotations should suffice to illustrate the position.

> Women, in the course of the present century, have officially become citizens in virtually every country of the Western world and in much of the rest of the world as well. From being totally relegated to the private sphere of the household, they have become enfranchised members of the political realm. However, women are increasingly recognising that the limited, formal, political gains for the earlier feminist movement have in no way ensured the attainment of real equalities in the economic and social aspects of their lives. Though women are now citizens, it is undeniable that they have remained second class citizens. Measured in terms of characteristics traditionally valued in citizens,

such as education, economic independence, or occupational status, they are still far behind men.[60]

[T]oday, women, though enfranchized citizens, are handicapped by the fact that neither their socialization nor their training, neither the expectations placed on them nor the opportunities or rewards afforded to them in their adult lives are such as to enable them to achieve economic, social, or political equality with men. The traditional, supposedly indispensable, nuclear family is used as the connecting link by which the basic biological differences between the sexes are expanded into the entire set of ascribed characteristics and prescribed functions which make up the conventional female sex-role. It is the definition of women in terms of their wife-mother role that continues to be used . . . to justify many kinds of discrimination against them, particularly in the sphere of education and employment.[61]

Motherhood in our society really does involve surrendering economic power and, with it, full adult status. Being 'separate but equal' is not a possible strategy for women under capitalism. . . . [T]he market forces of capitalism have simultaneously loosened and consolidated the sexual division of labour. Women are 'free' to work alongside men in the labour market, but not 'free' of the family commitments that have an overriding effect on their work lives.[62]

Within modern feminist parlance, both the putative system of male domination of women and of female subordination to men, as well as the sexual division of labour which is its immediate cause, have acquired names of their own. The former is called 'patriarchy'; the latter 'the sex-gender system'. Expressed in this terminology, therefore, the feminist complaint against classical liberalism is that, through permitting the perpetuation of the sex-gender system, the form of societal order favoured by classical liberals remains patriarchal in essence.

In order for women to enjoy justice and to gain release from their subordination to men, latter-day feminists argue that government must do more than simply discharge the functions of the minimal nightwatchman state proposed for it by classical liberals. A wide panoply of further legislative measures is deemed necessary. These range from government providing free universal child-care and equal mandatory paternity, as well as maternity, rights, requiring a reduction of the working day sufficient to permit parenting to be combined with full-time work, to relieving mothers of all economic dependency on the fathers of their children through the state taking over the task of financing the upbringing of children.

Suppose we understand by the term 'feminism' that movement which seeks to advance the welfare and interests of women. Then, as in the case of liberalism, we can distinguish two forms of it, classical and modern. Classical feminism maintains that the well-being and interests of women are best promoted through women being accorded the same set of civil and political rights as men are in the liberal form of order. By contrast, modern feminism maintains that, where accorded none but these rights, women remain subjected to injustice and subordinate to men.

Modern feminism rests on one crucial assumption. This is that any traditional sexual division of labour that is able to survive in the liberal form of order is inherently disadvantageous to women. This assumption, however, is by no means self-evident. It requires some substantiation before the case for modern feminism can or should be granted. When challenged to substantiate it, feminists are liable to cite in its support the fact that women tend to earn less than men, tend to own less of society's wealth, and tend to be disproportionately under-represented in society's most prestigious and powerful positions.[63]

Such statistical disparities between men and women, however, by no means suffice, on their own, to establish that the sexual division of labour which generates them is inherently disadvantageous to women. They can do so only upon two further assumptions. The first is that, on full and informed reflection, women would prefer to enjoy strict parity with men in such matters, plus whatever social alterations would be necessary to bring it about, to whatever currently prevents them from achieving it. The second is that the civil and political rights that a liberal polity accords its members are insufficient by themselves to enable women to achieve such parity with men, should they prefer to enjoy such parity to what they must forfeit to achieve it.

In order to determine the validity or otherwise of modern feminism, it is necessary, then, for us to answer the following pair of questions. First, is it true of all female members of modern liberal societies that, on full reflection, they would prefer strict parity with men in respect of occupational status at the cost of forgoing whatever prevents them from enjoying it? Second, are the set of rights accorded all members of a liberal polity insufficient to enable women to achieve parity with men, should they prefer it?

We know what in the opinion of modern feminists prevents women from enjoying such parity. It is the sexual division of labour. This makes child-care the primary responsibility of women and makes providing for children and for their primary carers the primary responsibility of men. Consequently, our questions must now be recast as follows. First, is it true of all female members of liberal societies that, on full reflection, they would prefer to enjoy parity with men in respect of occupational status, at the cost of forgoing being the primary carers of their children, to being their children's primary carers at the cost of forgoing parity with men in terms of occupational status? Second, are the rights accorded individual members of a liberal society insufficient to enable those women who wish it to enjoy such parity with their male counterparts, at the cost of ceasing to be their children's primary carers and the fathers of their children ceasing to be the primary providers for them?

No doubt, many of those who call themselves feminists would, on full reflection, prefer to enjoy parity with men in respect of these positions to being the primary carers of their children. However, this by no means shows that *all* women *do* or *would*. But suppose some, or even all, female members of a liberal society were to prefer parity with men in employment and politics to being the primary carers of their children. It still does not follow that there is anything about the rights accorded members of such societies which prevents women from obtaining such parity, if that is what they want. So, let us review these matters in turn.

The modern feminist case relies, in part, on the contention that, on full and informed reflection, women would prefer to enjoy parity with men in terms of occupational status to being the primary carers of their children. Many modern feminists profess to having such a preference themselves, and also impute it to other women. But there is considerable grounds for being sceptical of both these claims. This is so, at least in the case of any female member of a liberal society who has been the primary carer of her own pre-school children. Consider those modern feminists who profess to having or having had this preference. One is entitled to enquire whether they were their children's primary carers during the pre-school years of these children. If they were, one is entitled to wonder which more accurately reveals their considered preferences: their actions or their words. Only if something *prevented* these women from not being primary carers might the fact they were such carers not reveal that to have been their preference. Whether anything did is something we shall investigate presently. If they were not themselves the primary carers of their own children, one is entitled to enquire upon what basis they claim a liberal society prevents women from not being their children's primary carers.

So far as other women are concerned, there is considerable evidence to suggest that most, if not all, become their children's primary carers through *preference* rather than from lack of choice. Studies have revealed that women who become mothers exploit their qualifications to obtain jobs that permit them to become or remain the primary carers of their children when their qualifications would have enabled them to gain jobs with sufficient earnings to purchase substitute care.

Married men with the most earnings capacity also exploited it most effectively, working longer hours and more resourcefully the more education and credentials they possessed. By contrast, the more earnings capacity commanded by married women the less they used it. In other words, the more education and credentials possessed by a married woman the less likely she is to work full time at a highly demanding and remunerative job.

Later statistics confirm the general pattern. . . . Women seek education and credentials chiefly in order to gain more time with their families, while men seek these qualifications in order to earn larger incomes and provide for their wives and children. . . . Such differences in behaviour amply explain the differences between male and female earnings without any recourse to discrimination.[64]

More than this, there is evidence to suggest that women are genetically predisposed to have a stronger attachment to their young children than do their fathers.[65] This suggests that, within a two-parent family in which the parents initially start out with approximately equal inherent earning capacity, it will be to the mutual advantage of both parents, other things being equal, for the man to concentrate more on income-generation and the mother on child-care, for as long as it is necessary that at least one parent be the child's primary carer. In view of these considerations, there is good reason to greet with some scepticism the feminist claim that women would, on full reflection, prefer parity with men in terms of occupational status to being the primary carers of their children.

Grounds for such scepticism are strengthened when one turns to consider what precisely is supposed to be preventing women in a liberal polity from ceasing to be their children's primary carers and from achieving parity with men in the field of employment, should such parity be what they want. It is a constant lament of modern feminism that, notwithstanding the fact that, within the liberal form of order, they enjoy the same set of civil and political rights as men, women are still unable to gain parity of power and status *vis-à-vis* men. Their inability is claimed to stem from the extra demands made on their time and energy by being expected to be their children's primary carers and men their children's primary providers.

What has to be considered, however, is precisely what, within a liberal order, supposedly prevents women, should they want, from being able to achieve parity of economic and political status with men. The main alleged culprits would appear to be primarily two in number. The first is sex-role stereotyping, in other words, socialization. The second alleged culprit is sex discrimination in employment. So far as sex-role stereotyping is concerned, children of both sexes are brought up so as to internalize different conceptions of what role is to be expected of them as adults *vis-à-vis* child-rearing. Girls are brought up so as to consider it their role to be primary carer, rather than primary provider or dual-parent. Boys are brought up so as to consider their role to be primary provider. So far as concerns sex-discrimination in employment, in a liberal order, employers are at liberty to and will have incentive to discriminate against women in job selection. This is because women will be judged greater risks than men in consequence of their greater liability to cease full-time employment upon becoming a parent. Work-places in consequence tend to be organized by and for full-time males, rather than those who combine work with child-rearing responsibilities. Consequently, because women tend to be primary carers, they will enjoy fewer opportunities to advance in the workplace than men.

The question is whether, in a liberal society, either sex-role stereotyping or sex discrimination in employment would be sufficient by themselves or in tandem to prevent women, should they wish, from achieving parity of occupational status with men at the cost of relinquishing their traditional role as their children's primary carers.

Evidently, *if* women did wish for such parity, it would follow that the sex-role stereotyping that had supposedly gone on in their case would have failed to be as effective as feminists claim it is. Had socialization been as effective as feminists claim it to be, those women would presumably never have acquired any such unfeminine desire. Consequently, should women have the desire for occupational parity, it follows from the mere fact they have the desire that sex-role stereotyping cannot be sufficient to prevent women from achieving it.

Let us then turn to the claim that, in the form of order advocated by classical liberals, the ability of employers to engage in sex-discrimination in hiring would prevent women from attaining such parity, even should they want it. So far as this claim goes, two points may be made. First, there is little evidence to suggest that, in selecting and promoting, employers do discriminate against women on grounds of sex *per se*. The evidence comes in the fact that the earnings gap between men and equally well-qualified women who do not have children is negligible.[66] Consequently, the decisive factor is here is the division of labour that a couple who have children effect between themselves, *vis à vis* providing and caring for their children, rather than discrimination by employers.

There would appear to be nothing in a liberal society to stop women who wish to achieve occupational parity with men *demanding* as a condition of having children with them that their male partners share these responsibilities equally. What it makes sense for a couple to do in terms of dividing up between them the tasks of income-earning and caring for their children depends upon their respective earnings capacity. Suppose it turns out that it makes more economic sense for one to remain in full-time employment and the other to withdraw temporarily from the labour-market to concentrate on full-time child-care. And, suppose, further, that women have a stronger wish, or a weaker aversion, than men have to engaging in child-care. In such circumstances, for couples of otherwise approximately equal earnings capacity, the traditional sexual division of labour is likely to be their mutually most preferred arrangement. However, this is a matter for them, not their employers.

The second point is this. Suppose it should be the case that, in the form of order which classical liberals advocate, sex-discrimination in employment takes place, as it is permitted to do, at least, within the private sector. Suppose male employers, for whatever reason, prefer to hire, for a given wage, men rather than, as well or even better qualified, women. Then, the field would left wide open for women to out-compete these male-chauvinist firms in the market-place. This is so, in virtue of the equal or superior skills of the women passed over by sexist employers. The non-sexist or anti-male firms which hired the more talented women should be able to undercut or out-perform their competitors. As has been observed by the economist Robert Higgs, '[t]he most effective way to eliminate discrimination is to make all markets as competitive as possible. Competitive markets place costs of discrimination on discriminators far more readily than any other alternatives, certainly far more readily than a political alternative'.[67]

The conclusions to which we are ineluctably driven are as follows. There are no good reasons for supposing that, in the form of societal order advocated by classical liberalism, the rights accorded women are insufficient to enable them to enjoy as favourable innocuous lives as any for which they might wish. There is no good reason to suppose that, provided due recognition is made for individual differences, there is anything disadvantageous to women in girls and boys being brought up so as to consider perfectly natural and proper the traditional sex roles in which they have different but complementary parental functions. Nor is there any reason to suppose that, were women to wish for themselves a role other than the traditional one in which they are expected to be primary carers of their children, there is anything to prevent them from being able to assume such a role, through private agreements between themselves, their spouses, and the employers of both. Finally, there is no reason to suppose that, were male employers to be prejudiced against hiring women on grounds of merit, those women passed over as a result of prejudice would not be able to be as successful as their talents merited they be.

This completes my review of the modern feminist objections to the liberal form of order. With this, my review of the entire spectrum of modern liberalism is completed. I have argued that none of the animadversions of modern liberals against the order favoured by classical liberals survives critical scrutiny. Although the form of order favoured by classical liberals emerges unscathed from its encounter with modern liberalism, it faces fresh challenges from those who are as happy to reject modern as classical liberalism. In the next chapter, we consider the first of two sets of such challengers, the so-called communitarians. It is to their challenge to classical liberalism we now turn.

4 Communitarianism

4.1 THE COMMUNITARIAN CASE AGAINST THE LIBERAL POLITY

Classical liberals maintain best for all human beings that form of political regime which I have termed *the liberal polity*. To all its sane adult members, this form of polity accords a measure of liberty that permits them to do whatever they want, provided no one but at most themselves would be harmed by their doing it. The purpose of the present chapter is to review a particular line of objection to this form of societal order which has acquired considerable currency in recent years within academic circles. And not only in academic circles. Of late, this theme has been taken up within the British Labour Party.[1] The line of objection indicts the liberal polity in the name of community and in the name of two further sets of *desiderata* claimed dependent upon this first one. These are, first, the virtues as conceived of by the Aristotelian tradition of ethics, and, second, moral attitudes and beliefs that admit of rational justification.

Because of the importance they attach to community, these critics of the liberal form of societal order have come to be called *communitarians*.[2] A fundamental contention made by them is that a liberal polity is not and cannot be a community in their sense of the term. Nor, save at its margins, is this form of societal order at all congenial to other, more local, forms of community. Among those local forms of community which communitarians claim to be imperilled by the liberal polity are neighbourhoods, towns, cities, and ethnic and religious affiliations.[3] Hence, it is on two main counts that communitarians indict the liberal polity. First, they claim it deprives its members of the benefits of community. Second, they claim it deprives them of scope for the Aristotelian virtues as well as for moral beliefs which admit of rational justification.

These communitarian claims constitute a serious challenge for classical liberalism. If correct, they amount to a massive indictment of the liberal polity. But are they correct? This is what the present chapter seeks to ascertain. I shall focus primarily on that formulation of the communitarian position presented by Alasdair MacIntyre in his book, *After Virtue*.[4] My reason is that his book presents the first, fullest, and most detailed statement of the communitarian position, as well as being the most influential. I shall, however, from time to time refer also to the writings of other prominent communitarians, notably, Michael Sandel.[5]

There are two main theses about the liberal form of societal order which MacIntyre is most at pains to establish. The first is that this form of order is not itself a community. The second is that, because it is not a community, the members of one lack occasion for acquiring and exercising the virtues as well as rationally justifiable moral beliefs and attitudes.

Michael Sandel no more considers the liberal form of order a community than MacIntyre does. But what is more emphasized in the writings of Sandel than in MacIntyre's is the baneful effect which this form of order is alleged to have upon more local forms of community.

The procedure I shall adopt for carrying out my review of the communitarian case will be as follows. For each of the three *desiderata* with which communitarians claim the liberal polity to be incompatible, I shall first identify the specific reasons why these *desiderata* have been claimed by communitarians to be incompatible with a liberal polity. Having identified these specific reasons, I shall evaluate their strength.

4.2   COMMUNITY AND THE LIBERAL POLITY

As previously remarked, regarding community itself, communitarians make two fundamental claims in connection with the liberal polity. The first is this form of polity is not itself a community in their sense of the term. The second is that this form of polity is inhospitable to local forms of community within it. Save at its margins, such genuine forms of local community wither and die in a liberal polity.

In order to evaluate these two claims, it will be necessary first to answer three preliminary questions. First, what conditions must some form of human association fulfil for it to constitute a community as communitarians conceive of one? Second, whatever these conditions are, why do communitarians maintain a liberal polity to be incapable of satisfying these conditions? Third, why do communitarians maintain the liberal polity uncongenial to local forms of community? Only after all these questions have been answered shall we be in a position to assess the strength of the communitarian claim that the liberal polity deprives its members of the good of community.

First, then, how do communitarians conceive of community? What conditions do they maintain a form of human association must satisfy to be one? It would make for an easier and more economical discussion if it were possible to appeal to some clear statement in any of their writings of what they understand a community to be. Unfortunately, no such statement is to be found. From MacIntyre's text, however, a distinct conception of community may be extracted. It is to some such conception of community that he seems to be tacitly appealing throughout his work. Something like this conception of community seems to be common to all communitarians.

The conception of community that MacIntyre – and other communitarians – appear to be employing is the following. *A community is any form of human association in which every member experiences concern for and pursues the good of every other member as well as their own.* My textual warrant for attributing this conception of community to MacIntyre and other communitarians is as follows. As with other communitarians, MacIntyre treats the Greek *polis* as a paradigm case of a community in the relevant sense. More accurately, what MacIntyre considers a paradigm case of community is the Greek *polis* as he claims Aristotle conceived of it. Or, perhaps yet still more accurately, MacIntyre's paradigm case of a community is what he claims Aristotle conceived of the Greek *polis* to be ideally capable of being. Not only was the Greek city-state a community in this sense, we are also given to understand by MacIntyre that so too were medieval kingdoms. He tells us what made them all so. It was that, within each of them, their members together pursued *the* human good and not merely their own particular private good.[6] Such forms of association, we are further told, were ones in which the members were 'united in a shared vision of the good for man'.[7]

How do the characterizations of MacIntyre's of the Greek *polis* and of the medieval kingdom bear out the validity of my attributing to him that conception of community which I have? To see how, begin by considering precisely what MacIntyre could mean in this context by the expression *the human good*. Each individual member of one of these communities is said by MacIntyre both to have pursued his or her own individual good, and, of course, to have been human. It must follow that the human good which each is being said to pursue in addition to their own good must be some human good *other* than their own. But what could this other human good be? Of both the Greek *polis* and medieval society, it strains the imagination to suppose that it is MacIntyre's view that, in addition to their own individual good, every member pursued *the* good of any set of human beings more extensive than that constituted by every other member of their society. Consequently, in claiming that, in these societies, each member pursued *the* human good and not just their own, MacIntyre may be interpreted as claiming that, within these societies, each member pursued the good of every other member as well as their own good.

It must be admitted that it strains the imagination only somewhat less to suppose that, in the case of any actual societies of either of these two types, every member felt a concern for and pursued the good of every other member. Nevertheless, the possession of such a sentiment by members of a society is, I believe, constitutive of its being a community in the view of communitarians. The passages from MacIntyre quoted above are certainly consistent with this having been his conception. Admittedly, however, the passages cited so far do not compel us so to construe them. To confirm my interpretation, we must look to additional remarks of MacIntyre's about the ideal Greek *polis* as he maintains it was conceived by Aristotle.

MacIntyre claims that Aristotle's notion of the (ideal) Greek *polis* was that of a political community that was 'a common project'[8] for its members. By this, MacIntyre tells us, he means that its members were bound to one another in a form of 'friendship . . . which derives from a shared concern for goods which are goods of both'.[9] This claim of MacIntyre's suggests that, in order for some form of human association to count as a community in his sense, among the conditions which he thinks it must satisfy is the following: *every member must share with every other member a concern for goods which are the goods of every other member.* He also describes this form of friendship as 'the sharing of all in the common project of creating and sustaining the life of the city'.[10]

These passages reveal that, in MacIntyre's view, what made the Greek *polis* a community in his sense was its possessing the following two features. First, every member was bound to every other member through a tie of friendship which involved each in possessing a concern for goods for which every other member also possessed a concern. Second, the creating and sustaining of the life of the city was a project in which every member participated.

Besides the good of every other member besides themselves, for which good could every member of one of these societies share a concern with every other member? We are told that, in the *polis*, everyone participated in the project of creating and sustaining the life of it. But what is to be understood by the expression, 'the life of the *polis*'? By this term, it seems not unreasonable to understand nothing other than the life of its members as members. It would then follow that MacIntyre is claiming of the *polis* that every one of its members had a concern for and pursued the good of every other member, as well as for their own good, by participating together in the common project of creating and sustaining the lives of the members of the *polis*.

Recall, now, that MacIntyre has also said that in the *polis* every member shared a vision of the good for man. It follows that, on his view, what made the *polis* a community was that, as well as pursuing and having a concern for their own individual good, every member also pursued and shared a concern for the good of every other member. Hence, we arrive at the conception of community which I have attributed to MacIntyre.

Confirmation that a similar view of community may also be attributed to other communitarians can be obtained from the editorial introduction to a recent anthology on this tradition of thought, *Communitarianism: A New Public Ethics*. Here the editor, Markate Daly, enquires as to what the criteria are which mark the quality of relationship we associate with community. Daly answers the question as follows:

> There is fairly wide agreement on this: a community is composed of a limited set of people who are bound together in networks of relationships; the members share a set of beliefs and values; the relationships are personal and unmeditated, usually face-to-face; friendship or a sense of obligation, rather than self-interest, holds the members together; the ties among members encompass the whole of their lives rather than only one or a few aspects; members feel a sense of belonging – a sense of 'we-ness'; the interests and identity of each member intimately depends on and forms that of the whole; and members demonstrate solidarity with one another.[11]

This accords closely with the conception of community I have claimed is derivable from MacIntyre's writings. From now on, I shall also assume that the conception of community that I have attributed to MacIntyre is held by all communitarians.

Having now understood what MacIntyre and other communitarians understand community to be, we can embark on our two main tasks. The first is to consider the reasons that are offered by communitarians for denying a liberal polity to be a community in their sense. The second is to consider what their reasons are for claiming the liberal polity to provide an inhospitable environment for other more local forms of community.

It is overwhelmingly clear what, in the view of communitarians, ultimately precludes the liberal polity from being itself a community. It is the measure of *individualism* which it is taken to license its members. By the term, 'individualism', in this context, I mean the pursuit of self-interest. The measure of individualism which a form of societal order licenses is inversely proportionate to the amount of legal compulsion for members to attend to and pursue the interests of other members besides themselves. A liberal polity merely prohibits its members from harming one another in various ways. Save for those for whom, by some voluntary act, a member may be considered to have assumed special responsibility, this form of polity does not legally compel any member to assist any other member.

The liberal polity, thus, licenses its members to refrain from attending to and pursuing the good of any other member. It is clear why in MacIntyre's view a liberal polity is not a community in his sense of the term. It is because it does not legally compel its members to assist one another positively. Two quotations from MacIntyre should be sufficient to confirm the accuracy of attributing this view to him.

The notion of the political community as a common project is alien to the modern liberal individualist world. . . . We have no conception of such a form of community concerned, as Aristotle says the *polis* is concerned, with the whole of life, not with this or that good, but with man's good as such. . . . From an Aristotelian point of view a modern liberal political society can appear only as a collection of citizens of nowhere who have banded together for their common protection. They possess at best that inferior form of friendship which is founded on mutual advantage. . . . They have abandoned the moral unity of Aristotelianism.[12]

[W]hat the medieval kingdom shares with the *polis*, as Aristotle conceived it . . . [is] that both are . . . communities in which men in company pursue *the* human good and not merely as – what the modern liberal state takes itself to be – providing the arena in which each individual seeks his or her own private good.[13]

It is also clear that it is the same large measure of individualism which the liberal polity is taken to license which Sandel maintains renders it destructive of local community. Two illustrative quotations from Sandel should suffice to confirm the accuracy of this claim.

Communitarians worry about the concentration of power . . . in the corporate economy . . . , and the erosion of . . . intermediate forms of community.[14]

A way of life that seems to be receding in recent years [is] a common life of larger meanings, on a smaller, less impersonal scale than the nation-state provides. . . . Contemporary liberalism lacks a . . . communal strand. Its predominant impulse is individualistic. . . . The nation is too vast to sustain more than a minimal commonality, too distant to permit more than occasional moments of participation. Local attachments can . . . engage the[se] citizens in a common life beyond their private pursuits. . . . The anxieties of the age concern the erosion of those communities intermediate between the individual and the nation, from families and neighbourhoods to cities and towns to communities defined by religious or ethnic or cultural traditions. . . . Under modern conditions, . . . the growth of corporate power . . . leave[s] local communities to the mercy of corporate decisions made in distant places. . . . The greatest corrosive of traditional values are . . . features of the modern economy. . . . These include the unrestrained mobility of capital, with its disruptive effects on neighbourhoods, cities, and towns; the concentration of power in large corporations unaccountable to the communities they serve; and an inflexible workplace that forces working men and women to choose between advancing their careers and caring for their children.[15]

We have now identified the communitarians' conception of community. We have also identified their reasons for denying the liberal polity to be one, as well as their reasons for claiming this form of polity to be an inhospitable environment for local forms of community. In the next section, we consider the validity of these various claims about the liberal polity.

4.3   THE LIBERAL POLITY, INDIVIDUALISM AND THE GOOD OF COMMUNITY

The preceding section identified what, in the view of communitarians, prevents a liberal polity from being able to confer upon its members the good of belonging to a community. It was the amount of individualism and indifference towards others legally licensed by this form of polity. It is thus clear upon what the validity or otherwise of the communitarian indictment of the liberal polity turns. It turns upon the accuracy of their estimate of the magnitude – and of the effects upon local communities – of the measure of individualism licensed by such a form of polity.

The first point to be made is that *communitarians grossly exaggerate the magnitude of the measure of individualism licensed by the liberal polity*. MacIntyre maintains that measure to be so extensive as to permit members to pursue *merely* their own private good. Sandel claims this measure is such as to render large corporations *unaccountable* to the communities they serve. Both of these claims are literally false.

So far as MacIntyre's claim is concerned, no liberal polity can or would permit any of its members to pursue *only* their own good. This is so, for two reasons. First, every liberal polity imposes legal restrictions on the pursuit of self-interest by its members. No one is permitted to pursue their private good in ways that harm others. Second, the measure of liberty to pursue their own good which a liberal polity licenses its members is always such that, for every member, each is best able to pursue their own good only through pursuing the good of others. Within a liberal polity, there is no more effective way for any member to pursue their own good other than by cooperating with other members in ways which each considers advantageous to themselves. Accordingly, within the liberal polity, each individual member typically pursues his or her own good by engaging in some activity that aims at promoting the good of some other member(s).

As regards Sandel's claim, no liberal polity can or does permit corporations to be unaccountable to the communities they serve. First, the ultimate community which a corporation serves is not the work-force of that corporation, or the local communities from which that labour-force is recruited. It is, rather, the customers of these corporations. Corporations which do not take their customers into account in what they produce and in the prices at which they offer what they produce to them would very soon not have any and be forced to shut down! Wherever corporations do have customers, then, this is because these corporations are taking the communities they serve into account!

In response to this objection to his claim, Sandel would, no doubt, reply that the set of customers of any corporation does not form a community in his sense of the term. But suppose that the communities which Sandel is more likely to have had in mind in making his claim were the local communities to which the local labour-force of some corporation belonged, rather than its customers. It would still be false that corporations are unaccountable to these communities within a liberal polity. First, no company would be permitted to pollute the local environment, or at least such part of it as was privately owned by anyone other than the corporation. This would include the lungs and skin and other bodily organs of local residents as well as their physical property. Pollution is a form of harm to others that a liberal polity would prohibit. Second, in a liberal polity, no corporation would be at liberty to shut down plant in an area without honouring any contracts drawn up between itself and the work-force recruited from that area. It is true that, in a liberal polity, a corporation would be permitted to move from an area the prosperity of which has previously been heavily dependent upon the employment which that corporation provided in the past. However, the fact that a liberal polity would permit corporations to move with resultant local unemployment does not show that corporations which do move with this effect are unaccountable to these local communities. It no more shows this than, were the members of these local communities to move *en masse* to some other employer, who offered them more favourable terms, their doing so would render them unaccountable to the corporations which previously employed them. Corporations and local community are as accountable to one another as they contract to be. To suggest that corporations should be accountable to their local communities to any degree greater than that which the liberal polity requires them to be stands in need of an argument that Sandel fails to supply.

What about the accountability of corporations to their shareholders? Presumably, where corporations wish to shut down plant and relocate, this is out of considerations of profit. Corporations are accountable to their shareholders. The latter have funded the corporations or have bought shares in these companies from those who did, in the expectation of the corporation making profits for them. Individuals would not fund corporations in the first place, or purchase shares in them subsequently, other than for the sake of sharing in the profits they expect and hope the corporations will make for them. Suppose that, out of consideration for the local community in which its plant had been previously been located, a corporation failed to move where it would be more profitable for it to be located. For a corporation not to move for such a reason would be for its management to be guilty of a serious breach of trust to their shareholders for the sake of people to whom the corporation did not have any such contractual obligation.

At this point, it is open to communitarians to reply that, for a corporation to be subject to account to its shareholders rather than to its local community, is precisely an instance of the measure of individualism sanctioned by a liberal polity which they consider so pernicious. But consider what the alternative would be to a system of corporate financing which gave corporations license to move in this way. Not only would customers of corporations be less well served. It is also more than likely that there would exist fewer and smaller corporations and as a result fewer people would be employed and thereby capable of raising families of their own. In the absence of corporations being at liberty to move from considerations of profit, everyone would be less well-off. This includes those local communities which temporarily suffer reduced circumstances when corporations move which have formerly provided them with employment opportunities. In addition, one is entitled to wonder precisely why the company was obliged to move. Were labour costs lower elsewhere? If so, had the workers in the plant that was shut offered to reduce their wages to keep it going?

The upshot of the foregoing considerations is this. The measure of individualism licensed by a liberal polity is not nearly as extensive as communitarians commonly claim it is. Communitarians might concede this, yet still maintain that it is nonetheless sufficiently extensive as to preclude from being a community in their sense any polity in which it was licensed. I shall now argue that, *even were the members of a liberal polity to engage in that full measure of individualism licensed by it, this need not necessarily preclude that polity from being a community in the communitarians' sense*.

It will be recalled that, as we have construed it, the communitarian conception of community is of an association in which each member pursues, and is concerned for, the good of every other member as well as for their own good. The maximum measure of individualism that a liberal polity licenses its members is exclusive concern for, and pursuit of, their own individual good, subject to one very important proviso. Their pursuit of their self-interest must not involve harming any other member. In order for members of a liberal polity to exercise no more than this measure of individualism, each would have to be concerned to avoid harming others in pursuing their own good. Such harm-avoidance constitutes a form of concern for, and pursuit of, the good of other members. Admittedly, it is a form of concern for others of only a very rudimentary and limited kind. Still, the need for every member to avoid harming others means that the liberal polity is not a state of nature. Rather, it is a community according to our construal of the communitarian conception of one.

Suppose that the members of a liberal polity were to show no more concern for the good of other members of that polity than merely to avoid harming them. It must be conceded that they would fall considerably short of displaying that degree of concern for fellow members that it is more customary to think of members of a community having for one another. But, then of course, in practice, members of a liberal polity customarily concern themselves much more fully with the good of fellow members than merely seeking to avoid harming them in their individual conduct. This is especially so where the liberal polity in question is a democracy. Where members of a liberal polity are given opportunity to vote in general elections, they are given ample opportunity to become concerned with the good of the life of their polity in a way that altogether goes beyond their merely seeking to avoid harming any other member in their individual conduct. They can, and are encouraged to, become concerned about which candidates are best for society as a whole. Typically, voters in liberal democracies do not vote simply and solely in terms of what is best for themselves. Rather, they vote in terms of what is best for their society as a whole. This is arguably because most voters think that what is best for society as a whole is also best for themselves. Consequently, where a liberal polity is a democracy at least, nothing precludes it from being a full community itself in the communitarian sense.

Suppose it is granted that, since members of a liberal democracy *need* not vote in elections, there is nothing about this form of polity *per se* which necessitates it be a community, in anything but the most attenuated of senses. It is clear that, in consequence, a liberal polity *might* fail to be a community itself in all but the most attenuated of senses. Even so, *the fact that, in all but the most attenuated of senses of community, a liberal polity might itself fail to be one does not suffice to establish that the measure of individualism it licenses renders it inhospitable to as many and various other forms of community as every member might need to be able to enjoy as good a life as they might.*

In other words, assume that, in order for someone to lead a life as good as any which they might, it is necessary that the individual have the opportunity to enjoy the good of community with others. Assume, also, that the measure of individualism licensed by a liberal polity permits this form of polity itself not to be such a community. Even so, the fact that a liberal polity *need* not itself constitute one such form of community does not preclude all its members from all being able to enjoy within it as much community as each might need to lead a life as good as any which they might have.

Let us grant that being a member of a community is an indispensable condition of someone's enjoying a life as good as they could. Only if one or other of the following two propositions were true would a liberal polity be unable to guarantee its members scope for as much community as any might need for a life as good as any they might have. The first of these two propositions is that participation in the political life of one's polity is an essential component of enjoying as good a life as one can. The second proposition is that, in licensing that measure of individualism which it does, a liberal polity is bound to lead to the erosion and eventual destruction of all those forms of community in which it is necessary for someone to participate in order to enjoy as good a life as he or she can. If either or both these propositions were true, it would follow that the liberal polity could not be the best form of political order. However, neither would appear to be true.

Consider, first, participation by an individual in political life of the polity of which that individual was a member. There is no reason for supposing that, in order for anyone to enjoy a life as good as any they might, it is *necessary* that they engage in such a form of activity. There is nothing about political activity *per se* which necessitates that someone *must* engage in it in order to enjoy as good a life as any which they might. It is, indeed, desirable that members of a liberal polity have the vote. This enables them to replace in a peaceful way governments they do not find

satisfactory. But this only makes political participation a contingent instrumental good. In any case, all that is necessary to keep a government from
abusing its power is that the members of a polity have the periodic power
to vote it out of office. It would not be necessary for them all to exercise
that power.

Some communitarians often give the impression that there is something
so profound and wonderful about participating in the political life of one's
community that a liberal polity stands condemned because it does not
ensure that every member does so participate. However, they produce no
grounds for this claim. Let us concede that, in a less attenuated sense of
community than that in which a liberal polity must necessarily be one,
membership of some form of community is undoubtedly good. This does
not mean that, to enjoy the good of community in full measure, everyone has to participate in the political life of their society. Aristotle, whose
authority seems to count high with some communitarians, certainly did
not think any such thing. Aristotle's view was that the best possible human
life was not that of the statesman or politician but that of the philosopher.
The good of community was attainable by philosophers through their sharing
and participating together in the common pursuit of wisdom. This form of
community provided philosophers with as full and authentic a form of
community as they needed for as good a life as they could have.[16] We can
reject the proposition that it is a necessary condition of someone's well-
being that they participate in the political life of their society.

The validity of the communitarian claim would thus appear to turn
on whether a second proposition is true. This, it will be recalled, is the
proposition that the measure of individualism licensed by a liberal polity
is necessarily so destructive of local forms of community as to leave the
members of one with insufficient scope for as much community as they
each need to enjoy lives as good as they might have. Can this claim be
made out? I do not believe communitarians have provided any reason for
supposing that it can be. As we have seen, Sandel attempts to establish this
claim by citing in its support the damaging effect which private corporations can have on local communities when they move out of these areas.
I earlier argued that companies being at liberty to move in this fashion
does not entail that they must be considered unaccountable to these
communities in any degree. But I do not wish to deny that Sandel is correct that local communities can, at least in the short term, suffer the consequences of such corporate action. What I want to consider, however, is
what follows from the fact that a liberal polity licenses such sorts of corporate action.

Does it follow that this form of polity is necessarily so destructive of local community as to leave members of one with less scope for community as they might need to enjoy lives as good as any which they might enjoy? It is not clear to me there is any reason to suppose this. Suppose that, as a result of a long-standing local employer moving, a local community suffers acute unemployment. There is no reason for thinking that the relocation of a corporation that previously provided members of a local community with employment must render the members of that local community any less able to display towards one another anything less than full concern for one another's good. As Charles Murray has pointed out,[17] what is far more likely to erode such care and concern for one another in the members of a local community is where basic forms of service become provided by the state. In such circumstances, individuals think they need not bother to be concerned for the good of their neighbours because it is being taken care of by the state. Communitarians fail to establish that the measure of individualism licensed by a liberal polity necessarily deprives its members of sufficient opportunity for as much community as any might need for a life as good as any they might have.

Of course, in licensing that measure of individualism that it does, a liberal polity makes it theoretically possible for every member to become so preoccupied with their own good as for there to be no genuine community between them in any full-blooded sense. Should that be so, their lives might well be less good than they would have been had their society been less individualistic. But what exactly is supposed to follow from this fact? Let us assume that, if members of a liberal polity were to be as individualistic as their polity licensed them to be, they would as a result fail to enjoy as much well-being as they might otherwise be capable of. Let us further assume that, in any society which licensed a lesser measure of individualism than does a liberal polity, its members would be less individualistic than they are at liberty to be in a liberal polity. From these two assumptions can it be inferred that a liberal polity is less able than are more communitarian ones to provide members with the benefits of full-blooded community membership? The answer is: no. For, as I have argued earlier, there is nothing inherent about the liberal polity that precludes community in the full-blooded sense of the term.

It is true that the measure of individualism licensed by this form of polity could, theoretically, result in the absence of any form of community among its members in the full blooded-sense of the term. However, it is one thing for a liberal polity to license such a measure of individualism. It is an altogether different thing for a liberal polity to *compel* its members to engage in such a measure of individualism. That a liberal polity licenses a measure of individualism that would, if exercised in full, preclude community does not mean this form of polity *compels* its members to be that individualistic. It may thus be conceded that membership of community in a full-blooded sense is an indispensable component of a life as good as anyone might have. It may further be conceded that the measure of individualism licensed by a liberal polity could preclude its members from enjoying community in any such full-blooded form. However, from the propositions conceded, it cannot be inferred that a liberal polity is any less able than forms of societal order less individualistic than it to provide its members with the benefits of community in a full-blooded sense. For a liberal polity does not compel, but only permits, its members to be individualistic to the point at which they would forfeit the benefits of full-blooded community membership. This being so, the liberal polity might still be capable of providing its members with greater scope for full-blooded community than does any other societal form. This is in fact the view of such classical liberals as Hayek.

Hayek has described as 'the silliest of the common misunderstandings' of individualism 'the belief that individualism postulates (or bases its arguments on the assumption of) the existence of isolated or self-contained individuals, instead of starting from men whose nature and character is determined by their existence in society'.[18] Hayek has pointed out that classical liberalism always rested its case for the liberal polity upon its claim that this form of polity will foster strong and vigorous forms of local voluntary community. Hayek writes

> [Individualism's] emphasis is on the fact that . . . the state . . . ought . . . to be only a small part of the richer organism we call 'society' and that the former ought to provide merely a framework within which free (and therefore not 'consciously directed') collaboration of men has maximum scope. . . . This entails . . . that the deliberately organized state on the one side, and the individual on the other, [are] far from . . . the only realities, while all the intermediate formations and associations are to be suppressed. . . . True individualism affirms the value of the family and of all the common efforts of the small community and group. . . . [I]t believes in local autonomy and voluntary associations, and . . . indeed its case rests largely on the contention that much for which the coercive action of the state is usually invoked can be done better by voluntary collaboration.[19]

The outcome of our discussion so far is this. MacIntyre and other communitarians have not established that, by licensing as extensive a measure of individualism as it does, the liberal polity is bound to deprive its members of the benefits of community membership. Therefore, in appealing to the good of community, communitarians have failed to provide any sound reason to suppose that this form of polity is any less able than are any other forms of polity to supply its members with the benefits of community.

I now turn to a second communitarian charge against the liberal polity. This is that, in licensing as extensive a measure of individualism as it does, the liberal polity deprives its members of scope to acquire and exercise the virtues as these moral character traits have been understood within the Aristotelian tradition of ethics.

4.4 THE LIBERAL POLITY, INDIVIDUALISM AND THE VIRTUES

A central thesis of MacIntyre's is that, with the exception of those who continue to belong to traditional forms of community which, he claims, are capable of surviving only at the margins of one, a liberal form of societal order must deprive its members of scope and reason to acquire and exercise the qualities deemed to be virtues within the Aristotelian tradition of ethics. This thesis of MacIntyre's is grounded by him on two other claims he makes. The first is a claim about what provides human beings with scope and reason to acquire and exercise these qualities. The claim is that the possession and exercise of these qualities better enables their possessors to participate in a certain range of forms of life. The second claim is that the measure of individualism licensed by a liberal polity – particularly within the economic sphere – undermines and destroys all the forms of life for which possession of the Aristotelian virtues is needed or advantageous.

Our task is to appraise the validity or otherwise of MacIntyre's thesis concerning the fate of the Aristotelian virtues within the liberal polity. To do this, it will be necessary to identify and then assess the force of the considerations which he adduces in support of each of the two claims upon which he bases it. Several questions need to be answered. First, for being able to participate in precisely which forms of life does MacIntyre consider the Aristotelian virtues necessary or advantageous? Second, in precisely what ways does MacIntyre consider the measure of individualism licensed by a liberal polity to be destructive of these forms of life? Third, besides their better enabling their possessors to participate in these forms of life, might not individuals have independent reason for acquiring and exercising the Aristotelian virtues, reasons which could obtain even within a liberal polity which lacked these forms of life? I shall now proceed to answer each in turn.

According to MacIntyre, there are three varieties of life-form which provide human beings with scope and reason for acquiring and exercising the Aristotelian virtues. He respectively designates these by the terms *practices, life-as-a-narrative-unity*, and *traditions*. MacIntyre explains what he means by 'a practice' as follows.

> By a 'practice' I am going to mean any coherent and complex form of socially established cooperative human activity through which goods internal to that form of activity are realized in the course of trying to achieve those standards of excellence which are appropriate to, and partially definitive of, that form of activity, with the result that human powers to achieve excellence, and human conceptions of the ends and goods involved, are systematically extended.[20]

A good internal to a practice is one the achievement of which by someone, even where the outcome of competition, 'is a good for the whole community who participate in the practice'.[21] The examples which MacIntyre gives of goods internal to practices include the innovations in seascape painting effected by Turner and the development of new and more effective techniques of batting introduced into the sport of cricket by the batsman, W. G. Grace. Their innovations are said to have 'enriched the whole relevant community'.[22]

Goods that are internal to some practice contrast with those which MacIntyre calls *external*. Of external goods, so MacIntyre claims, it is characteristic that 'when achieved they are always some individual's property and possession. Moreover characteristically they are such that the more someone has of them, the less there is for other people.'[23] The examples given by MacIntyre of external goods are power, fame, and money and wealth.

Besides the game of cricket and painting, MacIntyre cites a number of other forms of activity as instances of practices in his sense. These activities include other games of skill, for example football and chess, various fine arts, including the art of architecture, the sciences such as physics, chemistry and biology, and the work of the historian.[24]

MacIntyre also informs us that another important form of activity is also a practice in his sense. He writes that

> in the ancient and medieval world the creation and sustaining of human communities – of households, cities, nations – is generally taken to be a practice in the sense in which I have defined it. Thus the range of practices is wide: arts, sciences, games, politics in the Aristotelian sense, the making and sustaining of family life, all fall under the concept.[25]

The second variety of life-form for engaging in which MacInytre deems the Aristotelian virtues to be an advantage is that which is said to consist in someone's life having *a narrative unity*. Of this form of life, we are told that it consists in a life being lived out by someone, in part, as a moral quest to discover what is the good for themselves personally and good for man *per se*. He writes that 'it is the systematic asking of these two questions and the attempt to answer them in deed as well as in word which provides the moral life with its unity. The unity of a human life is the unity of a narrative quest.'[26]

The third variety of form of life for which MacIntyre claims possession and exercise of the Aristotelian virtues to be either an advantage or necessary are those he calls *traditions*. A tradition is some historically enduring and socially transmitted way of going about engaging in one or more of the other two varieties of forms of life. Traditions are said to be perpetuated in one or other of two ways. The first is within and by means of the communities into which human beings are born and from which they derive their identities. These include families, tribes and nations. The second is by means of and within institutions, such as universities, farms and hospitals.

In MacIntyre's schema, *institutions* are not themselves practices. This is so, despite practices not being able to exist for long without supporting institutions. Unlike practices, we are told, institutions are always concerned with the acquisition and distribution of those external goods needed in order for any practice to go on. Even games of chess, typically, require a board and pieces!

According to MacIntyre, 'when[ever] a tradition is in good order it is always partially constituted by an argument about the goods the pursuit of which gives to that tradition its particular point and purpose'.[27] These arguments go on within the communities and institutions whose purpose and function it is to sustain and transmit these traditions. MacIntyre writes

> So when an institution – a university, say, or a farm, or a hospital – is the bearer of a tradition of practice or practices, its common life will be partly, but in a centrally important way, constituted by a continuous argument as to what a university is and ought to be or what good farming is or what good medicine is.[28]

According to MacIntyre, the qualities regarded as virtues within the Aristotelian tradition of ethics find their rationale in the contribution they make to successful participation in one or more of the forms of life of the three types mentioned above. Some of these virtues, such as justice, courage and honesty,[29] are deemed to be necessary in order to achieve the goods internal to any form of practice. This is so, if only because these qualities are needed in some measure by someone in order to be able to sustain with other participants in a practice those relationships without which it is impossible to engage in that practice.

> [W]e have to accept as necessary components of any practice with internal goods and standards of excellence the virtues of justice, courage and honesty. For not to accept these . . . so far bars us from achieving the standards of excellence or the goods internal to the practice that it renders the practice pointless except as a device for achieving external goods.[30]

A somewhat different rationale is given for other virtues, like constancy and integrity. They are said by MacIntyre to be needed to sustain the quest for the good which gives life its narrative unity. '[They] sustain us in the relevant kind of quest for the good, by enabling us to overcome the harms, dangers, temptations and distractions which we encounter, and which will furnish us with increasing self-knowledge and increasing knowledge of the good.'[31]

Still others are said to be needed by individuals to sustain 'those traditions which provide both the practices and individual lives with their necessary historical context'.[32] Justice, honesty and courage fulfil this role, as well as also being needed to enable their possessors to engage successfully in practices. But there are some virtues of which the rationale is said to be tied to traditions. These virtues are said to include 'having an adequate sense of the traditions to which one belongs or which confront one'[33] and a virtue that MacIntyre refers to as *practical reason*[34] but which, I believe, is more accurately referred to by the term *practical wisdom*. The latter virtue consists 'in the kind of capacity for judgement which the agent possesses in knowing how to elect among the relevant stack of maxims and how to apply them in particular situations'.[35]

We have now discovered which forms of life, according to MacIntyre, provide human beings with their sole rationale for acquiring and exercising the Aristotelian virtues. We must now identify the considerations which MacIntyre adduces on behalf of his claim that the liberal form of societal order deprives members of one of a reason to acquire and exercise these virtues.

In essence, MacIntyre argues that the liberal form of societal order removes from its members the rationale for acquiring and exercising the virtues in consequence of the license it gives them to pursue wealth. Thus, what MacIntyre considers to be inimical to the virtues is that same measure of individualism which he also claims is so destructive of genuine community. There are two ways in which economic individualism is said to be inimical to the virtues, a direct and an indirect way.

Economic individualism is deemed to be directly inimical to the virtues on the grounds that, in terms of acquiring the external goods which constitute wealth, it does not always pay to be virtuous. MacIntyre observes

[T]he possession of the virtues may perfectly well hinder us in achieving external goods [viz. riches, fame, and power]. . . . Notoriously the cultivation of truthfulness, justice and courage will often, the world being what it contingently is, bar us from being rich or famous or powerful. . . . We should therefore expect that, if in a particular society the pursuit of external goods were to become dominant, the concept of the virtues might suffer first attrition and then perhaps something near total effacement, although simulacra might abound.[36]

The pursuit of wealth is said to be indirectly inimical to the virtues through being said to be destructive of the various forms of life which provide human beings, on MacIntyre's schema, with the sole reason they can have for acquiring and exercising these qualities. MacIntyre argues that, with the rise of capitalism, both political activity and individual work ceased to be the practices they formerly were. This was a direct consequence of the measure of economic individualism that became licensed with the rise of capitalism.

It will be recalled that, according to MacIntyre, in both the ancient and medieval periods, the tasks involved in making and sustaining households and larger communities, even states, were regarded by all who engaged in them as practices in MacIntyre's sense. In other words, MacIntyre claims these tasks were undertaken for their own sake as common ends, and not purely instrumentally as means to some further set of purely private ends. MacIntyre's view is that the rise of capitalism brought an end to this way of regarding these tasks. These tasks ceased to offer a common end to all members of society, but became undertaken by them merely for the sake of their individual and separate private ends.

Consider, first, the effect which MacIntyre claims the rise of capitalism had on political activity. Before capitalism, so he claims, human beings engaged in the tasks involved in making and sustaining their political community for the sake of the flourishing community which these tasks were intended to bring about. The good of the community as a whole was something that was a good for all those who engaged in political activity. After the rise of capitalism, so we are told, all this changed. These tasks were no longer engaged in for the sake of what they led to. A flourishing community was not an end of those who engaged in political activity. It was merely a means to purely private ends. The good of the community as a whole was not something that was a good for those who engaged in political activity. MacIntyre observes that 'the medieval kingdom shares with the *polis*, as Aristotle conceived it [that] . . . both are conceived as communities in which men in company pursue *the* human good and not merely as – what the modern liberal state takes itself to be – providing the arena in which each individual seeks his or her own private good'.[37]

A consequence of this change which MacIntyre does not hesitate to note is that, in modern capitalist society, there is no longer any point or purpose for the virtue of *patriotism*. This is understood as allegiance and loyalty to one's government, as opposed to one's country.

> [T]he practice of patriotism as a virtue is in advanced societies no longer possible in the way it once was. In any society . . . which lacks genuine moral consensus, the nature of political obligation becomes systematically unclear. Patriotism . . . is characteristically exercised in discharging responsibility to . . . [one's] government. When . . . the relationship of government to the moral community is put in question both by the changed nature of government and the lack of moral consensus in the society, it becomes difficult any longer to have any clear, simple teachable conception of patriotism, . . . The modern state is not . . . a form of government . . . [that is] . . . necessary and legitimate.[38]

The same can hardly be said to hold true of the smaller community that is the family. Nor does MacIntyre say this. Even after the rise of capitalism, those who formed and sustained families of their own continued to do so for the sake of that to which these activities led, namely, the flourishing of their members. Nothing that MacIntyre says suggests that he thinks that the corrosive effect of capitalism upon practices extends to the family. However, there is one important way in which capitalism does subvert practices which has a bearing on the household. It relates to the effect which the rise of capitalism is said to have had upon work. In removing work from the land to the factory, capitalism is said by MacIntyre to have destroyed the character of work as a practice. He writes

> So long as productive work occurs within the structure of households, it is easy and right to understand that work as part of the sustaining of the community of the household and of those wider forms of community which the household in turn sustains. As, and to the extent that, work moves outside the household and is put to the service of impersonal capital, the realm of work tends to become separated from everything but the service of biological survival and reproduction of the labour

force, on the one hand, and that of institutionalised acquisitiveness on the other. *Pleonexia*, a vice in the Aristotelian scheme, is now the driving force of modern productive work. The means–end relationship embodied for the most part in such work – on a production line, for example – is necessarily external to the goods which those who work seek; such work too has consequently been expelled from the realm of practices.[39]

Besides politics and work, there are other former practices on which capitalism is said by MacIntyre to have had a destructive effect. In causing work to cease to be a practice, capitalism moved surviving practices, for most people, to the margins of social and cultural life in professionalizing these forms of activity. This had the consequence that, for the majority of non-professionals, engagement in these practices ceased to be central to their lives. 'Arts, sciences and games are taken to be *work* only for a minority of specialists: the rest of us may receive incidental benefits in our leisure time only as spectators or consumers.'[40]

Capitalism is said to have had a no less deleterious effect on that form of human life which consists in someone's making of it a narrative unity. It was made a unity, we may recall, by being a quest to know what is good for oneself and for mankind. 'To think of a human life as a narrative unity is to think in a way alien to the dominant individualist and bureaucratic modes of modern culture.'[41] MacIntyre does not elaborate. It is clear, however, that he thinks this way of living life is incompatible with the dominant individualistic and bureaucratic forms of modern culture.

Finally, claims MacIntyre, capitalism is inimical, and self-consciously and deliberately so, to traditions. He writes that '[t]he individualism of modernity could of course find no use for the notion of tradition within its own conceptual scheme except as an adversary notion'.[42]

One effect of this change in conception of the nature of political society, according to MacIntyre, is that the state no longer takes it upon itself to instil any of the virtues in its citizens other than law-abidingness. By contrast, before capitalism, the community was thought of by its members as more than an arena for the pursuit by each of their own self-chosen ends. Consequently, 'the political community not only require[d] the exercise of the virtues for its sustenance, but it is one of the tasks of political authority to make children grow up as virtuous adults'.[43] After the rise of capitalism, there is no longer any incentive to inculcate in its members any virtues besides that of law-abidingness. Within liberal capitalism, writes MacIntyre

a community is simply an arena in which individuals each pursue their own self-chosen conception of the good life, and political institutions exist to provide that degree of order which makes such self-determined activity possible. . . . Although it is the task of government to promote law-abidingness, it is on the liberal view no part of the legitimate function of government to inculcate any one moral outlook.[44]

We have now identified the reasons MacIntyre offers in support of his claim that the liberal polity is inimical to the virtues as conceived of within the Aristotelian tradition of ethics. It is time now to turn from exegesis to criticism. There are two questions which we must consider. First, how convincing are MacIntyre's grounds for maintaining the pursuit of wealth to be both directly and indirectly subversive of virtues such as justice and truthfulness? Second, how convincing are MacIntyre's grounds for claiming that the sole reason human beings have to acquire or exercise the virtues is to be better able thereby to participate in those various forms of life of which capitalism is said to be destructive?

We begin by considering how accurate MacIntyre's estimate is of how subversive of the virtues is that measure of economic individualism that became licensed by the liberal polity. MacIntyre's contention is that such virtues as justice and courage may hinder those who possess them in the pursuit of external goods. If such pursuit becomes dominant in a society, so he further claims, then the concept of the virtues will suffer attrition and near-total effacement. How much substance is there in either of these claims?

So far as the first is concerned, MacIntyre has anything but made out a case for it. It may perfectly well be conceded to MacIntyre that, as he says, the world being what it is, a commitment by someone to justice and honesty can, on occasion, lead them to forgo acquiring riches in circumstances in which they can do so through their performing some unjust or dishonest act. It does not follow, however, that, if someone attaches importance and value to the acquisition and possession of riches, he or she is thereby bound to be disposed to act dishonestly or unjustly. This remains so, even if, by acting unjustly or dishonestly, someone can thereby acquire greater riches than he or she otherwise could. Someone is only so disposed, if he or she attaches no higher value or importance to justice and honesty than he or she does to the acquisition and possession of wealth. MacIntyre has failed to provide any reason for supposing that those disposed to pursue wealth to the measure they are licensed to do by a liberal polity must either be or become incapable of attaching any higher value to moral integrity than to wealth. MacIntyre may be correct that, on occasion, someone can acquire greater wealth through acting unjustly or dishonestly. But he is wrong to have inferred from this truth that anyone who pursues wealth will always be predisposed to act unjustly and dishonestly in pursuit of it.

At this point, MacIntyre would no doubt claim that, unless someone participates in some form of life which gives virtues their point, no one can have motive or reason to prefer honesty and justice to wealth. All such forms of life, he would add, are destroyed by the unrelenting pursuit of wealth licensed by the liberal polity. To decide whether he is correct, we shall have to consider two issues. The first is whether wealth-pursuit is as subversive as MacIntyre says it is of those forms of life which, so he further claims, alone provide individuals with reason for acquiring and exercising the virtues. The second is whether, outside the context provided by these forms of life, individuals would have no reason to acquire and exercise any of the virtues.

MacIntyre has done anything but establish that wealth-pursuit undermines all those forms of life which he says provide the virtues with their rationale. There are several forms of life claimed by MacIntyre to be imperilled by the measure of wealth-pursuit licensed by a liberal polity. These include political life, work, the arts and sciences. None of the considerations which MacIntyre adduces in support of this claim about the deleterious effects of capitalism upon the character of these forms of activity is at all convincing. Consider, first political activity. Before capitalism, MacIntyre claims, political society was a community in the full-blooded sense with which we have become familiar in the previous section. This involves, we have seen, each member desiring and pursuing the good of every other member as well as their own. After the rise of capitalism, political society became merely a means to the private good of each member. Members of society ceased to desire the good of their society save as a means to their own private ends.

Suppose MacIntyre were correct that, with the rise of capitalism, human beings ceased to pursue or care for the good of their fellow members save as a means to their own good. It would not follow that political activity thereby ceased to be itself a practice in MacIntyre's sense. At most, all that would have happened is that fewer members of political society were obliged to engage in political activity. Whoever did would still have to be concerned and pursue the good of their community as a whole.

Consider, next, work. MacIntyre claims that, in being removed from the home to the factory, work becomes purely instrumental. When undertaken within the home, its connection with the household permitted work to be linked to the practice of making and sustaining one's family. However, neither the removal of work from home or farm to factory, nor work becoming commodity production, necessitates that work not be a practice in MacIntyre's sense. To illustrate this, consider, as an example, the production of motor-cars. The immediate goal of motor-car production is, let us say, the production of quick, safe, comfortable, and affordable means of transportation. The ulterior objective of such activity is the acquisition of wages and profits by car-workers, managers and shareholders. The immediate goal of motor-car production can perfectly well qualify for being considered a good internal to the activity in MacIntyre's sense. Even if engaged in for the sake of some ulterior purpose, such as income, an activity can still be a practice in MacIntyre's sense of the term. After all, MacIntyre cites as a good internal to cricket the development of a new batting technique. If the development of a new batting technique can count as a good internal to a practice, and professional cricketers are capable of developing new batting techniques, then so too can the production of a new range of motor-cars.

MacIntyre might care to deny that the production of motor cars can count as a good internal to the activity of motor-car production. He might claim that in order to be a practice an activity must be engaged in for its own sake, rather than for the sake of what it brings about. But this cannot be the case with all those activities which MacIntyre himself has cited as examples of practices. MacIntyre cites architecture as an example of a practice in his sense. But architects engage in the activity of architecture for the sake of the bringing into being of the buildings that they design. Similarly artists paint pictures for the sake of the pictures they paint being brought into being. But if productive activities can be engaged in for the sake of their products without these activities ceasing to be practices in MacIntyre's sense, why can they not be engaged in for the ulterior purpose of profit or wages without ceasing to be practices in this same sense? MacIntyre has provided no good reason for thinking that, where people engage in certain productive activities for the sake of income or profit, those activities are precluded thereby from being instances of practices in his sense.

Consider, next, that form of life which consists in someone's giving their life a narrative unity. MacIntyre claims that such unity is conferred upon the life of an individual by that individual treating it as a quest to discover the good of both themselves and others. He claims such a way of thinking of life is 'alien to the dominant individualist mode of culture'. But what grounds are there for thinking this? What possible features of the liberal polity render this form of quest *alien* to it? It may be granted that not everyone in a liberal polity will construe their life in this way. But this does not mean their so construing it is alien to the members of such a polity. To appreciate just how mistaken MacIntyre is about this, one need only think of the massive industry in modern capitalist societies dedicated to helping people 'discover' their own good and that of humanity. If anything, it is arguable that a liberal society may be said to be liable to prevent some of its members from realizing their good by enabling them to become too self-consciously preoccupied with the quest to discover what is good for them! And, this, of course, is to disregard the strength which more traditional ways of pursuing this quest in the form of organized religion continue to have within such societies.

As we have seen, MacIntyre claims 'modernity' to be incompatible with such traditions. But there is no more reason to follow him on what he says here about the effect of liberal regimes on life-forms of this kind than in what he says about its effect on the others. Consider for a moment how intensely a religious society the USA continues to be. What possible grounds can there be in view of this example for asserting modernity to be averse to tradition?

No one would deny that traditional life-forms have been subject to very serious erosion in recent years. One thinks most notably of the traditional nuclear family. But to what extent has the subversion of such institutions been the result of any of the forms of activity that would be licensed by the liberal polity? And to what extent has such recent subversion of these institutions occurred as a result of state-welfare measures which would be proscribed within a true liberal polity?

Suppose, however, that the measure of economic individualism licensed by a liberal polity were as subversive and destructive of forms of life as MacIntyre claims it is. Would it follow that, were members of a liberal polity without all these various forms of life, they would thereby cease to have reason to acquire and exercise the Aristotelian virtues? Within such a society would there be no other ends worthy of choice for which these qualities would be either necessary or an advantage? Were there to be at least one such end, then MacIntyre would be mistaken in maintaining the virtues to be compromised or subverted by the liberal polity.

Arguably, there is such an end. Moreover, it is one which is unmistakably in accord with the Aristotelian tradition of the virtues. This end is that of personal happiness! Nothing in what we have so far encountered in MacIntyre's arguments goes any way towards showing that possession and exercise of the Aristotelian virtues are not both necessary for the attainment of personal happiness. Nor have we so far encountered anything in his argument to show that the attainment of this end by an individual is impossible in the absence of those forms of life which, MacIntyre claims, are subject to destruction by the liberal polity.

Everyone always has good reason to have the attainment of happiness as one of their aims. Now, it is arguable that anyone who does adopt any such end for themselves will always thereby be provided with reason to acquire and exercise the qualities considered virtues within the Aristotelian tradition of the ethics. For the chances of someone being able to attain such a life must always be increased considerably by their possession and exercise of these qualities. This remains the case, notwithstanding the fact that, on occasion, a dishonest or unjust act can secure someone some external good which they might be otherwise unable to obtain.

As we shall see in the next section, MacIntyre does offer a set of considerations against appealing to personal happiness as a way in which to justify moral precepts to someone. He claims the notion of happiness is too indeterminate to be able to derive by appeal to it any guidance on how best to act to attain it. Suppose he is correct. It does not follow that appeal to it cannot be made to provide someone with reason to acquire and exercise the virtues. For it is arguable that a person's chances of being happy are always going to be increased in consequence of their possessing and exercising these qualities, even if one cannot say precisely in what their happiness will consist.

In response to this line of criticism, MacIntyre might want to protest that what he had in mind under the notion of the quest was pursuit of the end of personal happiness. But if he did, this is not what he said. It is one thing to lead a life which is as good as any one might have. It is another to be concerned to know which sort of life that is. My contention is that the Aristotelian virtues are needed by someone so that they may secure for themselves a life as good as any which they might enjoy. I did not wish to suggest that, in order for someone to enjoy such a life, they need be concerned to know which sort of life that was which is the object of the quest. This is not to say that a person can possess or exercise the virtues without their being concerned to know how it is proper and honourable for one to act. It is, however, to imply that a person can acquire the requisite moral knowledge, or at least the requisite moral belief, and thereby be able to live virtuously without needing to believe that their being virtuous is the most effective way of their achieving happiness.

At bottom, there is only one real argument which MacIntyre presents for his claim that in a liberal polity people lack reason to acquire and exercise the Aristotelian virtues. This is that, on occasion, it is possible for someone to obtain greater material wealth than he or she might otherwise be able to acquire through performing some unjust or dishonest act. But we have seen that this argument has no force. It establishes MacIntyre's desired conclusion only if something else is true besides it. It must also be true that to enjoy as good a life as possible a person needs as much material wealth as possible, regardless of how one acquired it. No serious advocate for liberal capitalism has ever thought such a thing! Accordingly, our conclusion must be that MacIntyre has provided no good reason for supposing the liberal polity to be at all subversive of the virtues.

4.5 THE LIBERAL POLITY AND RATIONAL MORALITY

As well as depriving its members of reason to acquire and exercise the Aristotelian virtues, MacIntyre also accuses the liberal polity of depriving them of moral beliefs and moral attitudes for which they can find or offer any adequate rational justification. The low estimate which MacIntyre has of the rationality of liberal moral sentiment may be judged from the following quotations.

> The nature of . . . moral judgement in distinctively modern societies [is] such that it [is] no longer possible to appeal to moral criteria in a way that ha[s] been possible in other times and places – and this [is] a moral calamity.[45]

> Liberal individualism . . . embodies the *ethos* of the distinctively modern and modernizing world, . . . and nothing less than a rejection of a large part of that ethos will provide us with a rationally and morally defensible standpoint from which to judge and act – and in terms of which to evaluate various rival and heterogeneous moral schemes which compete for our allegiance.[46]

> [W]e still, in spite of the efforts of three centuries of moral philosophy and one of sociology, lack any coherent statement of a liberal individualist point of view.[47]

It is on the basis of two other claims which he advances that MacIntyre denies that liberal moral sensibility admits of rational justification. The first is that rational justification of moral convictions and attitudes can only be given through reference to some conception of what he calls *the human telos*. By this, he means a conception of some worthwhile end or object of human endeavour and striving. The second is that the liberal polity is based upon a rejection by its members of all such conceptions. Our object now is to assess the strength of MacIntyre's case for these two various claims. To do this, we shall review and evaluate the strength of the considerations which he adduces in their support.

Moral judgements and attitudes commend and prescribe, or else condemn and proscribe, certain forms of conduct or else those who engage in these forms of conduct. Those who make moral judgements and adopt moral attitudes seldom consider them as being nothing more than their own personal preferences and tastes. To anyone who makes a moral judgement or who espouses a moral attitude, the judgement or attitude has an element of objectivity that distinguishes it from a mere expression of personal and subjective taste. This believed difference in status is reflected in the very linguistic forms of moral judgement as well as in the authority which they present themselves as having for those who make them. For those who make moral judgements, the various forms of conduct and character that these judgements commend and prescribe, or condemn and proscribe, appear to *warrant* or call for these judgements on them. But can this appearance of objectivity be held to be anything more than an appearance?

According to MacIntyre, there is only one way in which moral judgements can be anything more than the expression of the subjective and thereby ultimately arbitrary preference and taste of those who make them. The various forms of conduct about which these judgements are made must either advance or impede the attainment by human beings of some worthwhile goal of human endeavour. It is to such a goal that MacIntyre gives the name *the human telos*. Consider moral judgements which commend or prescribe certain forms of conduct. On his view, these judgements admit of rational justification only if there is some such goal for which the commended forms of conduct can be shown to be necessary or advantageous. Likewise in the case of moral judgements which proscribe or condemn conduct. They are capable of rational justification only if the proscribed conduct can be shown to impede the attainment of some such goal. If there genuinely is a human *telos*, then conduct which leads to its attainment is right and worthy of choice and the choice of such conduct is good. Those who choose this conduct are worthy of approval and commendation. This is especially so, if their choice has involved them in overcoming strong internal or external disincentives for making it. Likewise, if there genuinely is a human *telos*, then conduct which impedes the attainment of it is wrong, the choice of this conduct is bad, and those who choose such conduct are worthy of disapproval and condemnation. Again, this is particularly so in circumstances in which it would have been easy for them to avoid engaging in this conduct.

In the absence of a genuine human *telos*, moral judgements can be nothing more than an expression of the arbitrary subjective preferences of whoever makes them. This is so, no matter how independent and authoritative a person's moral judgement may appear to them. But is there a human *telos*? And, if there is, what is it?

MacIntyre distinguishes two different conceptions of the human *telos*. They have each been held at different times and in different societies. The first he rejects, the second he endorses. The first conception of the human *telos* is that which was first propounded by Aristotle. Aristotle is claimed to have derived it from his teleological world-view. On this view, not only human beings, but everything that came into being naturally, has a goal or end worthy of attainment by that entity. What the goal or *telos* of an entity is depends upon the *kind* of entity it is. So, the goal or end of an entity is fixed for it by its nature or essence. In the case of living organisms, their generic *telos* is the full development and exercise of their distinctive biological endowments. In the case of the animals other than man, their *telos*, therefore, is the attainment by them of full biological maturity. This is the state in which they are both able and disposed to reproduce further instances of their species.

The *telos* of man is no different from that of the animals, save in so far as man possesses certain potentialities which no other animal does. What distinguishes man from the other animals is his possession of *nous* or rational intellect. Accordingly, for Aristotle, the human *telos*, the worthwhile object of human striving, is the attainment by human beings of a fully developed rational intellect. Indeed, Aristotle equates happiness, or *eudaemonia* as he calls it, with the activity which results from the exercise of the fully developed rational intellect. Any such activity must assume one or other of two forms. The first and highest form of rational activity Aristotle calls *theoria*. It consists in contemplation of eternal and unchanging objects. In Aristotle's schema, these were the first mover or God, the objects of mathematics, and the heavens. Thus, for Aristotle, engaging in theology, pure mathematics and theoretical physics are all instances of *theoria*. According to him, engaging in these forms of activity is the most supremely worthwhile of human activities. It is solely for the sake of being able to engage more fully in these forms of activity that, ideally, all else should be pursued. The second type of activity that results from the exercise of the fully developed human intellect is that which Aristotle calls *politike*. Unlike *theoria*, this activity is practically, rather than theoretically, oriented. It consists in reflecting on which forms of constitution and laws are best for members of a polity in order for them to achieve or come closest to achieving *eudaemonia*. (It would not be too much of an exaggeration, I hope, to describe both the writing and attentive reading of the present book to be an exercise in *politike*.)

It was Aristotle's view that, in order for anyone to attain the ultimate goal of engaging in *theoria* or *politike*, it was necessary for them to have acquired and to have exercised all the various qualities which he identifies as virtues. Indeed, these qualities are deemed to be virtues by Aristotle precisely because of the contribution they make to the ability of their possessors to be able to attain this supreme goal of human endeavour.

The qualities recognized by Aristotle as virtues fall into two kinds as they relate to the intellect itself or to the subordination of the passions to the intellect. The first kind of virtue are intellectual virtues. Of these, there are two: *sophia*, or wisdom, on the one hand, and *phronesis*, or practical wisdom, on the other. Virtues of the second kind are the moral virtues. The moral virtues include courage, temperance, justice, liberality, and many others.

The two intellectual virtues are needed by a person to enable them to enjoy *eudaemonia*. For without *sophia* and *phronesis*, it is impossible for anyone to engage in *theoria* and *politike* respectively. The moral virtues, in Aristotle's view, make an indirect contribution to the achievement of this supreme end. They are dispositions to choose those forms of conduct which best enable someone to attain and preserve a psychic economy which will permit them to acquire and maintain *phronesis* and *sophia*. The acquisition and exercise of the moral virtues enables a person to avoid becoming diverted from this most worthy of objectives through being led astray through the appeal of lesser goods like pleasure, or the avoidance of pain, or the acquisition of honour and esteem. This, in essence, is Aristotle's conception of the human *telos*.[48]

In marked contrast with Aristotle's own conception of the human *telos*, MacIntyre presents – and argues for – a second conception of it. This second conception does not rely upon any form of metaphysical biology as Aristotle's is alleged by MacIntyre to have done. According to this second conception, what provides human beings with a worthwhile goal of endeavour is the specific social identity that each individual acquires in consequence of being born into the specific sort of community they have. Every individual born into a community acquires thereby a certain unique identity. They are child of certain parents, a member of such and such a particular nation or religious faith, and so on. Each of these factors goes to make up or constitute that individual's identity and none is acquired by someone through their having chosen it. Further, each such constituent of someone's identity – for example, their being the son of so-and-so, a member of the such-and-such nation, and so on – provides that person with a certain role which carries with it certain duties and obligations to others or self. Similarly, none of these duties is acquired through any *decision* on the part of those bound by them to be so bound. Accordingly, where human beings are born into communities which provide their members with an identity rich in roles of this sort, then these human beings will each have been provided with a *telos*. That *telos* consists in their attaining whatever will be achieved by their discharging the duties associated with the set of roles which are constitutive of their identity.

In the case of this second conception of the human *telos*, what role, if any, do the Aristotelian virtues play in the attainment of it? It is MacIntyre's claim that the Aristotelian virtues enable their possessors to fulfil the various duties bound up with the roles that constitute their identity. Accordingly, it is by reference to a human *telos* so constituted, that moral precepts and moral judgements can be rationally justified by and to those who have an identity so constituted for them.

Aristotle's conception of the human *telos* is rejected by MacIntyre on the grounds that it is dependent upon a discredited and implausible form of metaphysical biology. By contrast, the second conception of the human *telos* – which MacIntyre claims in many ways to be far older than Aristotle's – is not dependent on any such thing. However, so MacIntyre argues, this second conception of the human *telos* cannot survive the establishment of a liberal polity. For to recall, on MacIntyre's view, such a form of polity is not a community in his sense. Consequently, the form of life which goes on within one does not lead the members of one to acquire that form of self-identity which confers upon them any *telos*. In sum, where someone is born into a liberal polity, then, because the society is not a genuine community, the identity they acquire is not one which endows them with any such *telos*.

In liberal regimes, therefore, we find, according to MacIntyre, a peculiarly etiolated and impoverished conception of human identity. Human beings are conceived in abstraction from, and as ontologically prior to, any moral obligations or commitments or goals they might have. On this view, all such obligations and commitments are the product of decision or voluntary adoption by an individual. This view of man which MacIntyre claims to be peculiar to and distinctive of liberal polities is that which he and other communitarians call *individualism*, in another but related sense to that which I gave it earlier. By the term in the present context, MacIntyre explains he means a certain conception of man. It is a conception in which 'man is thought of as an individual prior to and apart from all roles . . . each of which has its own point and purpose: member of a family, citizen, soldier, servant of God'.[49]

Suppose that human beings so conceive of themselves. Suppose, also (and rightly so, in MacIntyre's view), that they are unable to subscribe to any form of metaphysical biology such as that to which Aristotle subscribed. In such circumstances, claims MacIntyre, they will necessarily be bereft of any conception of a human *telos* to which they can appeal in justification of any moral judgements they might make. Accordingly, it is precisely in such a condition which we should expect human beings to be within the liberal polity. It is MacIntyre's view, therefore, that a liberal polity will ensure its members lack any conception of a human *telos*. Such a form of polity merely provides its members with a framework within which each can pursue their own private and voluntarily chosen objectives. Consequently, there is nothing beyond their own private choices and subjective preferences that provides them with any ultimate worth-while goal. Lacking a conception of any human *telos* to which appeal can be made, it becomes impossible for members of a liberal polity to offer or discover any rational justification for their moral convictions. Their moral judgements become no more than mere expressions of their individual arbitrary subjective preferences, dressed up in the appearance of an objectivity which they cannot have for them.

MacIntyre purports to find confirmation for this thesis in a feature which he ascribes to moral controversies characteristic of contemporary liberal societies. This is their interminable character. That is, none of the parties to these controversies is alleged to be able to demonstrate to their protagonist the correctness of their own particular views.

There are, according to MacIntyre, several factors which account for the interminability of the moral controversies in modern liberal societies. All stem in one way or another from the absence within these societies of any conception of a human *telos* to which appeal can be made in support of moral judgements. Lacking any such conception, the protagonists in these debates are unable to provide justifications for their own moral views. Instead, such arguments as they advance for their moral convictions tend to terminate in appeal to rival first principles for which neither party can give any adequate justification but on which both parties cannot agree. Agreement is said not to be possible because the rival first principles employ what MacIntyre calls incommensurable concepts. By this he means, the moral concepts in question are of 'quite different kinds . . . such that we possess no rational way of weighing the claims of one against the other'.[50] MacIntyre claims that the concepts of moral rights and of utility are incommensurable with one another. He cites their being so to explain the interminable character of moral controversies about justice in which considerations of utility are opposed by considerations of rights.

Lacking any conception of the human *telos*, the moral principles and judgements in which such incommensurable moral concepts figure cannot admit of rational justification. Consequently, in the absence of such a conception, these moral concepts themselves *cannot* be anything but names of fictions. They are but chimera intended to fill the justificatory void left by the abandonment, without replacement, of any conception of the human *telos*.

Of both the concept of utility and of moral rights, MacIntyre makes this claim. He needs to make it, if he is to maintain his thesis that moral judgements in liberal societies are incapable of rational justification. For they are the standard moral concepts through appeal to which adherents of this form of polity seek to justify it. Utility is said to be too indeterminate a notion to be the name of anything real. And the existence of moral rights is said to be as incapable of being demonstrated as that of ghosts.

Some moral judgements made by some members of liberal societies make use of moral concepts derived from pre-modern traditions of moral thought. Examples of such concepts are said to be those of virtue and duty. Moral judgements employing such concepts once admitted of rational justification through appeal to some underlying conception of a human *telos* that informed these traditions. But they can do so no longer. The concepts which these moral judgements employ have become disconnected from the original teleological frameworks which provided them with their original rationale. As a result, the moral judgements in which moral concepts such as duty and virtue figure are said to have become incapable of being justified, and the moral concepts themselves become misunderstood by those who employ them.

MacIntyre claims this unhappy fate to have been suffered by both the notions of moral duty and of the virtues. In connection with the latter set of moral concepts, he says that, where any conception of the human *telos* has been abandoned, the value of the Aristotelian virtues ceases to be understood in terms of their enabling their possessor to attain some worthwhile end of human endeavour. Instead, they are thought of in one or other of two different ways. Either they are conceived as dispositions which enable their possessors to fulfil their moral duties in the face of egoistic disinclination. Or else they are thought to be expressions of passions and dispositions conceived as useful or advantageous to their possessors or others. The former corresponds to the Kantian conception of virtues, the latter to Hume's. Neither philosopher, maintains MacIntyre, understands the virtues for what they truly are. Their respective understandings of the virtues, as well as the qualities which they take to be virtues, merely reflect the parochial standpoint of modern liberal society masquerading as that of universality in the minds of those who so construe them.

It is, thus, as misconceptions of their subject-matter that MacIntyre understands those modern philosophical conceptions of morality which conceive of it as a system of rules needed to counter man's natural egoism, and which conceive of the virtues as dispositions to obey such moral rules.

Likewise, MacIntyre construes as a misconception of its subject-matter Hume's broadly utilitarian conception of the virtues as human qualities which are agreeable or useful, or both, to their possessors or others. Hume claimed to be providing an account of the virtues that held true for all human beings at all times. MacIntyre rejects Hume's theory of the virtues. He does so on the grounds of its being allegedly unable to account for why anyone could ever have considered virtuous those ascetic qualities which Hume called 'the monkish virtues', and which Hume himself condemned. Indeed, instead of having provided an account of the virtues that holds true of and for all human beings, MacIntyre claims that the standpoint from which Hume has judged certain qualities virtues, because useful and agreeable, is no more than that of his own limited circle. He writes

> What Hume identifies as the standpoint of universal human nature turns out to be that of the prejudices of the Hanoverian ruling elite. Hume's moral philosophy presupposes allegiance to a particular kind of social structure as much as Aristotle's does, but allegiance of a highly ideological kind.[51]

We have now completed our reconstruction of the considerations which MacIntyre offers in support of his thesis that members of liberal polities are bereft of rationally justifiable moral convictions and attitudes. We must now turn to an appraisal of the strength of his case for this thesis. There are two questions we must address. First, do moral convictions admit of rational justification only through appeal to some conception of a human *telos*? Second, must members of a liberal polity be bereft of any such conception?

So far as the first of these questions is concerned, there is every reason to agree with MacIntyre. Matters are very much otherwise when it comes to the second question. There is little to suggest that members and advocates of liberal polities must be unable to appeal to any conception of the human *telos* in justification of their moral attitudes, *including their attitude of moral support for the liberal polity.*

The classical liberals advocated the liberal polity through an appeal to considerations of the happiness of its members. Appeal to the same consideration is capable of being employed in justification of other moral attitudes and convictions. MacIntyre interprets utilitarianism as an attempt to devise for the rules of traditional morality a new teleology.[52] However, he claims that the notion of utility or greatest happiness is insufficiently determinate to be able to serve in this capacity. His reasons for this claim, however, are very weak. He writes the notion of human happiness is *not* a unitary, simple notion and cannot provide us with a criterion for making our key choices. . . . There are too many different kinds of enjoyable activity, too many different modes in which happiness is achieved. . . . Different pleasures and different happinesses are to a large degree incommensurable: there are no scales of quality or quantity on which to weigh them. Consequently appeal to the criteria of pleasure will not tell us whether to drink or swim and appeal to those of happiness cannot decide for me between the life of a monk and that of a soldier.[53]

The conclusion of this argument does not follow from its premises. There might well be, as Macintyre says there is, a great variety of different kinds of enjoyable activity and different modes in which someone might equally achieve happiness. Further, it might well be true that these different pleasures and modes of life are incommensurable with one another. Thus, it might be impossible for anyone to enjoy all these different types of activity and yet there be no neutral grounds on which one sort can be shown to be superior to the other. It may even follow from all this that appeal to considerations of pleasure or happiness is unable to tell an individual whether to choose between the life of a monk or a soldier. It does not follow from any of this, however, that, ultimately, the attainment of happiness is not a supremely worthwhile goal of human endeavour. Nor does it follow that appeal to considerations of what will promote or impede its attainment cannot be used to justify the commendation or condemnation of various forms of conduct. Considerations of pleasure may well be able to tell someone, who is suffering from a gastric ulcer, whether to drink or to swim! Likewise, considerations of happiness may well be able to tell a confirmed atheist whether to be a monk and to tell a devout pacifist whether to be a soldier! For those who are neither, perhaps appeal to happiness cannot provide guidance in a choice between these options. But then no philosophers who have recommended appeal to happiness in modern times as the ultimate standard in ethics have thought this notion would be able to offer such detailed guidance in the absence of a considerable amount of psychological detail. What appeal to considerations of happiness can do is justify rules of social living: some types of rule can be ruled out by appeal to the notion, and others can be judged more likely than other sets of rule to advance the well-being or happiness of a society's members.

It was reference to considerations of utility conceived in this broad sense which Hume maintained underlay our moral sentiments and hence which accounted for which human qualities were conceived of as virtues and which vices. We commend and admire those qualities the exercise of which would be liable to directly please or be useful to those who exercised them or to others. MacIntyre's grounds for rejecting Hume's account of the virtues do not establish their point. MacIntyre claims Hume's account cannot explain why certain ascetic qualities which are neither useful nor agreeable to anyone have been regarded by some as virtues. However, this is obviously mistaken. Those who regarded these qualities as virtues believed – albeit, no doubt, mistakenly, and certainly so in Hume's view – that these qualities were useful means for enabling their possessors to achieve greater piety or chastity, which qualities they further believed to be agreeable to God.

Consequently, MacIntyre fails to show that liberals cannot avail themselves of a perfectly serviceable notion of a *telos* to which they and members of liberal polities can appeal to provide rational justification for moral attitudes and convictions. This includes moral support for the liberal polity!

Exception may also be taken to MacIntyre's claim that contemporary moral controversies are interminable. We have already considered his grounds for this claim. It is that they employ rival moral concepts which are incommensurable with one another because they are either fictions or detached from their original teleological contexts. There is simply no reason for accepting any of these claims. The idea of rights is perfectly compatible with that of utility as I have argued in the chapter on modern liberalism. Moreover, notions of virtue and duty all admit of accommodation inside the broad utilitarian framework that informed the outlook of the classical liberals. Accordingly, the final result of our survey of the communitarian critique of the classical liberal view of which polity is best for human beings has failed to provide any convincing reason for doubting it.

5 Conservatism

5.1 VARIETIES OF MODERN CONSERVATISM

This chapter considers some recent critiques of classical liberalism made from a conservative perspective. What is distinctive about this perspective is something which those who adopt it find notoriously difficult to articulate. As its name implies, it is a political perspective which tends to value long-established political institutions and traditions, and which, therefore, tends to resist deliberately instituted change to them. But conservatives do not attach uncritical value to everything that exists. Nor are they resistant to all forms of political change. It is only towards long-established traditions and institutions that conservatives tend to feel affection. And, they are prepared to institute change to adjust long-established institutions to new circumstances, as well as to make radical political change in times of political instability and upheaval arising from long-established institutions having been subject to radical change by those unable to appreciate their value. The longevity of an institution is treated as *prima facie* evidence of its being satisfactory, and, hence, as *prima facie* grounds for resisting radical change to it.

What is distinctive about this perspective has been well immortalized in Michael Oakeshott's description of the conservative disposition. He writes

> The general characteristics of this disposition . . . centre upon a propensity to use and enjoy what is available rather than to wish for or to look for something else; to delight in what is present rather than what was or what may be. . . . What is esteemed is the present: and it is esteemed . . . on account of its familiarity. . . . If the present is arid . . . , then this inclination will be weak or absent; if the present is remarkably unsettled, it will display itself in a search for a firmer foothold and consequently in a recourse to and exploration of the past; but it asserts itself characteristically when there is much to be enjoyed, and it will be strongest when this is combined with evident risk of loss.[1]

Historically speaking, the political tradition known as Conservatism was born in reaction to and in protest against modernizing trends and tendencies championed by classical liberalism. Among these, the French Revolution is by far the most notable. It is only with the subsequent rise of socialism, from the mid-nineteenth century onwards, that conservatives and classical liberals acquired a mutual enemy against which to take common cause.

Each of the three political outlooks tends to regard its two rivals as more similar to one another than to itself. To socialists, conservatives and classical liberals defend unconscionable forms of privilege and inequality. It matters little to socialists whether inequalities be inherited and feudal or acquired through market transactions. To classical liberals, conservatives and socialists both favour governmental intervention in aspects of economic life better left to market transactions and voluntary association. Finally, to conservatives, socialists and classical liberals are wont to favour and engage in undesirable, because unnecessary, political reform and change. In the eyes of conservatives this misguided enthusiasm for change which afflicts both classical liberals and socialists stems from the folly of what, following Michael Oakeshott, many conservatives have come to call *rationalism*.[2] This is a tendency to subject established institutions and forms of order to incessant and needless critical scrutiny and reform in pursuit of political ideals which can seem attractive in theory but are unrealizable in practice. In place of such iconoclastic zeal, conservatives advocate respect and deference for establishment, tradition and authority. On this matter, in the eyes of conservatives, classical liberals are only slightly less guilty than socialists of rationalism in politics.

Unlike modern liberals, conservatives agree with classical liberals that there is nothing untoward about undeserved inequality *per se*. Again, like classical liberals – and in marked contrast with both communitarians and modern liberals – modern conservatives do not consider market institutions as *necessarily* corrosive of community and other important values.[3] Notwithstanding these points of affinity between conservatives and classical liberals, modern conservatives are no more happy with the liberal form of polity than are its other contemporary critics. In the case of conservatives, what is found objectionable about this form of polity is not its market economy. On the contrary, modern conservatives are as wedded as classical liberals to private ownership of the means of production, freedom of contract, and production for profit. This is so, at least in the case of societies in which these institutions and practices already exist. Where conservatives part company with classical liberals is over whether a polity that is possessed of no more than these institutions and practices, together with the other political and civil liberties offered by a liberal polity, is capable of providing human beings with as good a life as they can have.

In this chapter, I will focus on two recent conservative criticisms of the liberal form of societal order favoured by classical liberals. The first is that advanced by Roger Scruton.[4] The second, a more tempered and liberal critique, is that advanced by the self-styled post-modern liberal conservative, John Gray.[5] Each of these two critiques exemplifies a different tendency within modern conservative thought. Each alleges a somewhat different set of *desiderata* to be incapable of being provided by the liberal polity. What makes both critiques unmistakably conservative is the high regard in which each holds certain traditional values and forms of life deemed to be imperilled by the liberal polity.

5.2 ALLEGIANCE, PATRIOTISM AND NATIONHOOD

According to Roger Scruton, a liberal polity suffers from at least one major defect. It is, so he claims, unable to inspire and preserve among its members any *allegiance* or *patriotism*. Unless the members of a polity feel such sentiments towards it, its fundamental institutions will lack legitimacy in their eyes, its established traditions will not command their unquestioning support, and its laws and established government will cease to exercise any authority over them. Inexorably, without allegiance and patriotism being felt towards it, a political regime must cease to be able to reproduce and defend itself from internal decay and external assault.

Only under certain conditions are the sentiments of patriotism and allegiance said by Scruton to be able to arise in human beings. They have to be able to develop towards past and future generations of their society ties of loyalty and of self-identification. Scruton claims that the members of a society can identify themselves with and form ties of loyalty to other generations of members only when all sets of generations of members belong to the same nation as one another. Scruton is at pains to point out that, for two human beings to belong to the same nation as one another, it is neither necessary nor sufficient that they both be members of the same political society as one another. It is not necessary, since people can be of the same nation, yet be citizens of different states. This was true, for example, of the citizens of West and East Germany, prior to reunification. It holds equally as true in the case of citizens of the Republic of Ireland and Irish-Americans and of those Irish who have taken up residence in and citizenship of the United Kingdom. Likewise, it is not sufficient in order for two human beings to belong to the same nation as one another that they be members of the same state. Citizens of the same political society can belong to different nations from one another. This is true, for example, of the citizens of Switzerland, who, in terms of nationality, are either French, German or Italian. It is also true to a lesser degree of the citizens of both the United Kingdom and the United States.

Under what conditions, then, can two human beings be said to be of the same nation as one another? According to Scruton, what is required is that they share the same form of life as one another, where this is understood in a particular way. People share a form of life when and insofar as they share a common language, belong to the same associations, such as churches, schools and clubs, have a shared history, and have a common culture. Most notably, for Scruton, common nationality involves a shared religious affiliation. Only when the different generations of members of a polity share the same form of life with one another can there develop between them those ties of loyalty and identification on which their ability to feel patriotism and allegiance towards it is said to depend. Accordingly, in Scruton's view, the viability of any polity depends upon all generations of members of it belonging to the same nation as one another.

It is Scruton's claim that a liberal polity is unable to ensure that all its generations of members will share a common form of life. Because of this inability, the liberal polity is said to be unable to ensure that all its generations of members belong to the same nation as one another. The result, according to Scruton, is that a liberal polity is unable to sustain among its members that loyalty and allegiance towards it on which the viability of any form of polity depends.

What are Scruton's grounds for claiming that a liberal polity is unable to ensure that its members share a common form of life and hence belong to the same nation as one another? Essentially, they are that there is nothing about a liberal polity which requires that all its members belong to the same nation as one another. Nor, even when they all are initially, is there anything about a liberal polity which necessitates that all its subsequent members continue to belong to the same nation as one another. There is nothing in or about a liberal form of societal organization which prevents there from entering its territorial jurisdiction, settling there, and subsequently becoming members of it, immigrants who belong to some nation other than that to which its indigenous citizens belong. When large numbers of immigrants enter a society and continue to retain their traditional form of life within their new environment, they remain unassimilated. The members of the polity where they settle cease to belong to the same nation as each other, and the bond of unity on which patriotism and allegiance depend is broken.

It would seem that there is nothing a liberal polity can do to prevent national unity from being undermined through the immigration it must permit. More than that, in a world in which population and other natural resources are unevenly distributed, there is liable to be great economic incentive for members of some nations to settle in territories inhabited by members of other nations. This will occur whenever members of the former nations perceive the possibility of economic advancement in emigrating to these other countries. Such immigration is seemingly not to the disadvantage of members of the host nation. For there is seemingly considerable scope for mutually beneficial economic transactions between them. Even when working for lower wages than members of the host society would be willing to accept, immigrants from less economically developed coun-ies will still enjoy a better standard of living than they formerly did. In nsequence, then, it would appear that, not only is a liberal polity unable prevent such immigration from occurring, it is almost certainly likely to act it.

nmigrants who belong to a different nation from those of the host ty have already acquired full social identities of their own. Their pre-nt alien national identities will prevent them from being able to p towards other generations of the host polity anything like as strong of loyalty and identification as can and will be formed towards it by f its members who belong to the same nation as these other gen-of members. Undoubtedly, the children of first-generation immig-z form the requisite attachments, subject to their undergoing the te education and acculturation. But it would seem that, in a liberal ere is nothing to ensure – and, sometimes, much to prevent – the f first-generation immigrants receiving such an education. The is that a liberal polity is liable to weaken those pre-political ttachment upon which rests allegiance to it and its traditions. ing aptly summarizes Scruton's verdict upon the liberal polity.

liberal theory of the state' . . . makes no reference to historical ts or prescriptive obligations: government is legitimate only not dirty itself with the messy particularities of the flesh. . . . om – appearing . . . as the 'just society' of the contractarians our attachment to the realities through which we might, in condition, live and find fulfilment.[6]

nce, is Scruton's case against the liberal polity. Having now exposition of it, we may turn to its appraisal. The validity se rests upon his being correct in respect of three claims he t is that a form of polity can be a good one, only if it enables feel patriotism and allegiance towards it. The second is that olity can feel patriotism and allegiance towards it only if f its members belong to the same nation as one another. the liberal form of polity is unable to guarantee that all s members belong to the same nation as one another.

Scruton is undoubtedly correct in his first two claims, and for the reasons he gives. In order for a polity to be able to defend itself from external enemies and from subversion from within, it does seem necessary that its members feel patriotism and allegiance towards it. Therefore, no form of polity can be thought a good one which prevents its members from being able to acquire these sentiments. Likewise, people can be inspired to make sacrifices – and, in the case of war, the supreme sacrifice – only on behalf of those to whom they feel a loyalty and with whom they can identify. It further seems true that people are only able to feel loyalty to and fully identify with those with whom they share a common form of life in the sense of sharing a common language, association, history and culture. Given that people may be said to be of the same nation as one another when and only when they are linked by such bonds, Scruton is correct in maintaining that patriotism and allegiance can develop within a polity among its members only when they all belong to the same nation as one another. Scruton's strictures against the liberal polity will be justified, therefore, provided he is correct in the further claim he makes. This is to the effect that this form of polity is unable to ensure that all generations of its members be of the same nation as one another. On this crucial issue, however, Scruton fails to provide any compelling reasons to support his reservations about the liberal polity.

Why does Scruton doubt the capacity of a liberal polity to create and maintain common nationhood among all its members? It is because he doubts the ability of this form of polity to ensure that all its members share the same form of life, in the sense of sharing a common langauge, traditions, religion, and so on. Why does Scruton doubt the capacity of a liberal polity to ensure its members share the same form of life? It is because this form of polity is only a political form of union among its members. On Scruton's view, such a form of union between people cannot guarantee that they will share with one another a common form of life. Consequently for Scruton, a liberal polity cannot provide the necessary cultural basis for patriotism and allegiance. He writes

> The liberal state . . . generates no loyalty towards generations which being either dead or unborn, form no part of the [social] contract. Without such a loyalty, there is neither honourable accounting nor provision for the future, but only a squandering of resources in the pursuit of present goals. The liberal state must depend therefore upon some other loyalty than loyalty to itself. . . . Without loyalty to the dead, and to the land that houses them, the whole project of liberal politics is endangered. For a liberal state to be secure, the citizens must understand the *nation*

interest as something other than the interest of the *state*. Only the first can evoke in them the sacrificial spirit upon which the second depends.[7]

The validity of Scruton's strictures against the liberal polity turns on one issue. Is he correct that, in consequence of its being merely a *political* form of union, a liberal polity cannot ensure that its members share a common form of life, and hence together form a nation? In support of this crucial claim, however, Scruton is unable to supply any convincing grounds or evidence. What lends superficial credibility to it is that it is theoretically possible for a liberal polity to become host to a massive influx of immigrants of alien nationality to that of the host community and who choose to retain their alien identity by refusing to assimilate, even after having been granted citizenship. If the *only* point of similarity between the immigrants and the members of the host community were their all being citizens of and resident in the same state, then such immigrant communities would not be of the same nation as that of the indigenous population. However, when a polity is liberal in form, it is simply false, both historically and as a matter of conceptual possibility, that immigrants belonging to a nation different from that of the indigenous population can, for any significant length of time, remain unassimilated with the members of the host society in a way that makes of them all one nation.

As conceived by classical liberals, an immigrant ethnic minority simply could not function within a liberal polity without being able to converse with members of the host society. They are, thus, bound to acquire the capacity to speak the language of their host community. Likewise, in order to be able to survive, they are bound to have some dealings with members of the polity other than themselves. These will be forms of association with members of the host society, albeit rudimentary. Likewise, they are bound in time, although, perhaps, not in the first generation, to acquire the same history as that of the host community. This must happen as the polity is faced with common national crises and emergencies, such as wars or epidemics. As for a common culture, it is almost certain that, within time, it will be unavoidable for immigrants, or their children, to adopt the common culture of the host community, or at least as much of it as is needed to render them as unmistakably belonging to the same nation as that of the indigenous population. Scruton fails, therefore, to provide convincing reason in support of his claim that the liberal polity cannot meld into one nation members from a variety of cultural backgrounds and nationalities.

Additionally, there seems conclusive reason for rejecting Scruton's claim. As Scruton himself acknowledges, the USA is a classic case of a nation all of whose members emanate from a diversity of other nations. It is only,

perhaps, through having departed from the classic liberal ideals of its
founding fathers that has required it to impose stringent immigration con-
trols. Had it not done so, it would not have needed to restrict immigration.

Scruton professes to being able to find a source of philosophical support for his point of view in the political writings of Hegel. Scruton claims
that 'Hegel gives a succinct and complex warning against what may reasonably be described as the ruling fallacy of Victorian liberalism.'[8] The
following passage of Hegel's is cited by Scruton in support of his own
strictures against the liberal polity: 'If the State is confused with civil
society, and if its specific end is laid down as security and protection of
property and personal freedom, then the interest of the individuals as such
becomes the ultimate end of their association, and it follows that membership of the State is something optional.'[9]

Scruton places upon this passage of Hegel the following interpretation.
He claims that it is asserting that

> To take an instrumental view of government . . . is to re-cast the ties of
> citizenship and sovereignty as relations of interest, defeasible and extin-
> guishable in the manner of a business partnership. It is to neglect precisely
> that which makes obedience a habit, and civil association a profound
> ethical force: the transcendent authority of the political order.[10]

This interpretation of Hegel's passage seems unwarranted. By the expression, 'the state', Hegel did not mean what Scruton reads him as mean-
ing, namely, the government. As has been pointed out by Charles Taylor
among others, 'what Hegel means by "state" is the politically organized
community'.[11] The state, for Hegel, is, therefore, the entire polity. It thus
includes the families and all the other variety of voluntary associations
between members which unite them together in a common form of life.
When the polity is conceived of in this way, Hegel is surely correct that,
if someone does regard their polity solely as an instrument for their security, protection and freedom, he or she will regard their membership of it
as being something optional. But, *pace* Scruton, it does not follow that
Hegel viewed government other than as being instrumental. Nor does it
follow that viewing government as being solely instrumental prevents
obedience to it from being a habit or prevents civil association from having an ethical force. It is perfectly possible for members of a polity to have
an instrumental view of their government, while also possessing loyalty
towards past and future generations of members as a result of being bound
to them by ties of common nationhood.

In any case, Hegel is a dubious ally to whom Scruton should turn in
seeking support for his own views. The work of Hegel's in which Scruton

purports to find support for his own views is his *Philosophy of Right*. The preface of the work contains a severe attack by Hegel on a minor and now almost wholly forgotten German nationalist philosopher, Jacob Fries. Hegel attacked Fries for attending and addressing a meeting of a student fraternity in Warburg. At the time, there were many such student fraternities. In his study of Hegel's political thought, Shlomo Avineri supplies the following information about them. Avineri writes

> These fraternities pre-figured the most dangerous and hideous aspects of extreme German nationalism. . . . They were the most chauvinistic element in German society. They excluded foreigners from their ranks, refused to accept Jewish students as members and participated in the anti-semitic outbursts in Frankfurt in 1819. . . . The anti-rationalism, xenophobia, anti-semitism, intolerance and terrorism of the *Burschenschaften* [student fraternities] present the same syndrome which, under different circumstances, the Nazis were to institutionalize.[12]

Fries himself was a virulent anti-Semite and author of an anti-semitic tract entitled, 'On the Danger Posed to the Welfare and Character of the German People by the Jews'.

Avineri explains that in this pamphlet

> [Fries] accused the Jews of being the bloodsuckers of the people who contaminate the purity of life in Germany. He advocated the suppression of Jewish educational institutions, encouragement of Jewish emigration from Germany and prohibition of Jewish immigration into Germany. Laws should be enacted, Fries further suggested, to prohibit Jews from marrying Gentile; no Christian servants, and especially no maids, should be allowed to work for Jews, and Jews should be made to wear a distinctive mark on their clothes.[13]

In commenting on Fries's views, Hegel reveals that, for him, the modern state can be purely political in the sense of being founded on no more than the rule of law and what becomes possible on its basis. The political unity created by a *Rechstaat* is, thus, sufficient, in Hegel's view, for generating among its members those further ties between them which make them all one nation. Hegel comments on Fries's views that it is

> the quintessence of shallow thinking to base philosophic science not on the development of thought and concept but on immediate sense perception and the play of fancy; to take the rich, inward articulation of ethical life, i.e. the state, the architectonic of that life's rationality . . . and confound the completed fabric in the broth of 'heart, friendship and

inspiration'. . . . The special mark which [this school] carries on its brow
is the hatred of law. . . . The formal character of the right as duty and
a law it feels as the letter, cold and dead, as a shackle.[14]

It is clear from his remarks on Fries, that, for Hegel, the modern state
could and should be founded on law and nothing else. The loyalties and
attachments needed for allegiance and patriotism would, in his view, automatically develop in its members as a result of being citizens of such a
form of state. It is a mistake to think that Hegel of all philosophers thought
anything more than a proper legality was required for nationality.

The upshot of our discussion is this. While Scruton is correct that the
viability of a political society ultimately depends on its members forming
with one another a single nation, he is not correct in claiming that, in being
capable of being ethnically and culturally pluralistic, a liberal polity is necessarily inimical to the development of common nationhood among all its
members.

5.3   POST-MODERN LIBERAL CONSERVATISM

In marked contrast with Scruton, John Gray considers the pluralistic and
cosmopolitan character of present-day Western societies a given and unal-
terable fact about them. It is Gray's view that the multi-ethnic and multi-
cultural complexion of these societies makes it anachronistic and nostalgic
to hanker for a return of the mono-cultural form of nationhood demanded
by Scruton. We must accept a form of ethnic and religious diversity that
forever precludes, within modern Western societies at least, the creation
or restoration of forms of nationhood as culturally homogeneous as those
seemingly being advocated by Scruton.

Gray, however, is as concerned as Scruton with certain debilitating
effects which he, like Scruton, considers the liberal form of political order
can and does have upon its members. And, like Scruton, Gray is also of
the opinion that these defects will ensure that this form of polity will be
unable to command and retain the allegiance of its members.

At bottom, Gray denies that the liberal polity is best for all human
beings on the basis of three other doctrines for which he argues. The first
is a theory of the human good which Gray acknowledges to have derived
from Isaiah Berlin. To this theory, Gray gives the name, *radical value-
pluralism*. The remaining pair of doctrines on which Gray bases his case
against the liberal polity I shall explain presently. Both doctrines concern the degree of conduciveness of the liberal polity to the attainment by

members of one of the various forms of human well-being postulated by radical value pluralism.

The theory of radical value pluralism is itself comprised of two claims. The first is that there is such a variety of uncombinable and incommensurable human goods that there is no one single form of well-being or flourishing that holds true for all human beings. Rather, there is a variety of incommensurable forms of human well-being. Each consists in the attainment of some set of combinable human goods. Each of these sets of human combinable goods is incommensurable with any other set. There is, therefore, no rational way of demonstrating the superiority of any one of these forms of well-being to any other.

Human beings achieve well-being and flourish through attaining the goods belonging to one of these sets. However, it is by no means possible for human beings to attain every one of these forms of well-being. According to radical value pluralism, which specific forms of well-being are genuinely possible, for any human being, is a function of the kind of society in which that human being has been acculturated. Such a restriction is a consequence of the truth of the second constituent claim of radical value pluralism. This second claim is that human nature is so indeterminate, and, in consequence, human personality so much a social artefact, that a human being is only capable of those forms of well-being which are possible within that form of society in which that human being has been acculturated.

From the theory of radical value pluralism, Gray derives his conservative rejection of classical liberalism by conjoining with it two other doctrines. The first is that there is no form of human well-being for the attainment of which by every member of society a liberal form of societal order is sufficient, and only one for which a liberal form of order is necessary. The second is that, in the case of all other forms of human well-being (than that for which a liberal regime is necessary), these forms of well-being can only be attained in polities which are not liberal in form. Consequently, with respect to these other forms of well-being, liberal regimes preclude their members from attaining them.

An important corollary is derivable from the conjunction of this last doctrine with the second of the two constituent claims of radical value pluralism. The corollary is that, in the case of human beings who have not been acculturated within liberal regimes, not only is this form of regime not necessary for their well-being, but it can be positively inimical to it.

The sole form of human well-being for which Gray considers liberal political institutions to be necessary is that particular condition referred to by Gray as *autonomy*. Gray acknowledges Joseph Raz as the source of his account of this ideal of well-being.[15] By *autonomy*, Gray tells us he means

> the condition in which a person can be at least part author of his life, in that he has before him a range of worthwhile options, in respect of which his choices are not fettered by coercion and with regard to which he possesses the capacities and resources presupposed by a reasonable measure of success in his self-chosen path among these options.[16]

There are some human beings, Gray tells us, for whom autonomy is an essential ingredient of their well-being. In their case, a substantial part of that measure of liberty which a liberal polity accords them will be a necessary condition of their well-being. This is because liberal institutions – like political and civil liberty, private property, and individual freedom of contract – are necessary conditions of individual autonomy. These institutions and liberties are needed by these individuals to enable them to exit from and enter at will particular forms of life and activities and associations available to them and with which they have acquaintance.

Liberal political and economic institutions are, thus, acknowledged by Gray to be necessary for securing the well-being of those for whom personal autonomy is an essential ingredient of it. However, even in their case, argues Gray, liberal institutions are insufficient for enabling them all to attain well-being. This is claimed for two reasons. The first is that, in order for personal autonomy to be worth having, the options between which an individual has to be able to choose must each be choice-worthy. Gray claims that the institutional resources of a liberal polity cannot ensure that its members are provided with such a plurality of worthwhile options. Indeed, Gray claims that the institutions of a liberal polity are liable to be corrosive of many of these worthwhile options, thereby destroying the value of the autonomy it provides its members.

Gray's second reason for claiming the liberal polity incapable of supplying its members with everything they need for worthwhile autonomy is this. In order for a human being to enjoy personal autonomy, certain basic needs of theirs have to be satisfied. It is Gray's view that a liberal polity is unable to ensure the satisfaction of the basic needs of all its members. This will be the case for those members unable to provide for themselves because physically or mentally disabled, or else, though able-bodied, cannot find work. The institutional resources of a liberal polity are said by Gray to be insufficient to guarantee the satisfaction of the basic needs of all these unfortunates. They need supplementing with what Gray calls an *enabling welfare state*. This is a form of welfare-provision that could never be condoned by classical liberalism.

It is Gray's view that, in the case of those who live in pluralistic societies, such as the members of advanced Western societies, autonomy is an essential ingredient of well-being. Through their unavoidable exposure to alternative forms of life being practised within their societies, these human beings have been made aware of alternative ways of living. As a result, in their case, the ability to choose for themselves their individual particular form of life, from among the plurality of forms available to them, is an essential ingredient of well-being.

For those who have not grown up within such pluralistic societies, however, personal autonomy is not an essential ingredient of their well-being. Indeed, in their case, not only is autonomy not necessary for their well-being in Gray's view, what can often be necessary to it is the absence of the conditions needed for autonomy. This holds true, Gray wants to maintain, in the case of those human beings who have grown up in closed and hierarchical forms of society. Their identities will often have become such that their well-being is best served by their not possessing autonomy or the conditions for it.

In the case of all those who have not been acculturated within pluralistic societies, matters stand even worse for the liberal polity. Their socialization will have left them with identities and personalities such that they can attain well-being only within such non-liberal forms of life. In their case, in order that they enjoy as much well-being as they can, not only is it not necessary that their polities be liberal in form, it is necessary that their polities not be liberal. In the cases of such human beings, liberal institutions are positively inimical to their human well-being.

To illustrate his thesis, Gray offers a number of examples of members of societies of which he claims it to be true that, for their enjoyment of well-being, a liberal form of societal order is either unnecessary or downright inimical. These examples include members of feudal societies, such as medieval troubadours and courtesans, as well as members of contemporary Russian and East Asian societies. Members of the last-mentioned societies are admitted by Gray to have benefited greatly from the greater productivity which their adoption of market institutions has made possible. However, it is denied that they stand to benefit from their further adopting the political and civil liberties which have accompanied such market institutions in the West.

In sum, for Gray, the classical liberal project of seeking to promulgate the liberal polity throughout the world on the grounds of its being the best form of society for all human beings is misconceived. This project should be abandoned. At most, the liberal form of order has value only for those acculturated in modern pluralistic societies. Even then, such a form of order is not sufficient for the well-being of those for whom it is necessary. It needs modifying from its classical liberal form by having an enabling welfare state and social market economy.

Having now completed our account of Gray's critique of classical liberalism, it is time to turn from exegesis to criticism to ascertain how convincing it is.

5.4   RADICAL VALUE PLURALISM

It may readily be conceded to Gray that there exists a plurality of incommensurable and not always combinable human goods. Thus, to take an obvious example, it is not possible for someone to combine the life of a contemplative religious recluse (assuming, for the moment, such a life can allow someone a form of well-being) and that of a family man holding down a professional job in a large modern metropolis.

It may also be conceded to Gray that, since incommensurable human goods are not always combinable, there is a variety of distinct forms of human well-being between which human beings are sometimes obliged to choose. What need not be so readily conceded to Gray, however, is that all these various distinct forms of well-being are not all capable of being simultaneously attained, by different individuals of course, within one and the same polity. Nor need it be so readily conceded that a liberal polity is not that form of polity in which all the various forms of human well-being can be simultaneously attained.

How do Gray and Berlin support their claim that no form of polity is capable of accommodating within it every form of individual human well-being? What they appeal to is the fact that different forms of human well-being can be attained in a variety of ways not all of which are combinable with each other. However, this indisputable truth does not support the inference that Gray and Berlin draw from it. Let it be granted, as seems undoubtedly true, that it is not possible for there to be simultaneously realized within one polity all the various different *ways* in which all the different *forms* of human well-being can be attained. Thus, for example, it is not possible to have a society which combines the chivalric way of life of a medieval knight with that of a modern democratically elected political leader, assuming that both ways of life can instantiate different forms of human well-being.

From what has been granted, however, it simply does not follow that all the different *forms* of human well-being are incapable of simultaneous attainment within one polity. An analogy will make this clear. It is no doubt a fact – or at least could well be a fact – about each particular set of coloured surfaces on which the entire range of colours can currently be found that the members of each set cannot all be made congruent with one other. It does not follow from this that it is impossible to construct a set of congruent surfaces on which collectively the entire range of colours can be found.

In other words, Gray and Berlin fail to make an important distinction that needs to be made. This is the distinction between, on the one hand, *the distinct and different forms of human well-being*, and, on the other, *the distinct and different ways in which each of these forms of human well-being can be attained*. To illustrate the difference between the two things, consider the many different ways which a life of scholarly enquiry can assume, depending upon historical and other circumstances. Assuming such life can be a distinct form of human well-being, such a form of well-being can be exemplified in many different ways.

It would be true that not all forms of human well-being were simultaneously attainable within any one polity only if, for at least one of these distinct forms, there was no *way* in which it could be attained that could coexist with some set of ways in which each and all of the other forms of well-being could simultaneously be attained. In support of their thesis that the different forms of human well-being are not all co-possible within the same society, Gray and Berlin cite various cases of well-being that, they claim, could not coexist together. These cases show only that there are many distinct ways in which various different forms of well-being can be attained which are not all co-possible. The cases of well-being cited by Berlin and Gray do not show that all the different *forms* of well-being are incapable of coexistence with one another in some ways other than those ways which are mutually uncombinable. We may conclude, therefore, that neither Gray nor Berlin provides any reason for accepting the first of the two constituent claims that make up the radical value pluralism to which they both subscribe.

Berlin and Gray fail to establish the truth of the first claim of radical value pluralism. It might still nonetheless be true. It remains for us to consider, therefore, whether, in fact or of necessity, the various distinct forms of human well-being cannot all be attained through some set of ways which can all be accommodated together within the same form of polity and a liberal one at that. Once one distinguishes between a form of human well-being and a particular way in which some form of well-being can be attained, it becomes clear that there is no reason to doubt that all the several different forms of well-being can be simultaneously attained by means of some set of ways which are mutually capable of being accommodated with one another within some society.

Suppose, however, it were true that not all forms of human well-being were capable of co-existing with one another within the same form of society. It must then follow that the liberal polity would be incapable of accommodating within it every distinct form of human well-being that there is. However, even should that be so, it could still be true that membership of a liberal polity enabled every human being to attain a better life than did membership of any other form of polity. That is, a liberal polity could still be best, for every human being, even were not every form of human well-being attainable within it. For suppose a liberal polity enables every one of its members to attain *some* form of well-being, and suppose this form of well-being was, to each individual, as good as any other of which they were capable. Suppose, further, that no other form of polity was capable of doing the same. Then, even though some forms of human well-being might be irretrievably lost from history with the advent of universal liberalism, every human being might still gain from its advent, or at least some might unmistakably gain and none lose. Consequently, even were the first of the constituent claims of Gray's radical value pluralism true, his case for rejecting classical liberalism would be unsound, if the second of its constituent claims was false.

Conversely, suppose there exists some set of co-possible ways in which every distinct form of human well-being could be simultaneously attained. Suppose, further, that this set of ways were capable of being accommodated within a liberal polity, and only within such a form of polity. It would not follow that the liberal polity is best for every human being, if the second constituent claim of radical value pluralism were true. (This claim, to recall, is to the effect that human nature is so indeterminate and human personality so artefactual that human beings are only capable of attaining well-being in those ways that are possible within the specific societies with which they have been acculturated.) Were this claim true, then those who had already been acculturated within non-liberal regimes would, as a result of their acculturation, be incapable of attaining well-being in any of the ways made possible by a liberal polity. Consequently, notwithstanding the falsity of the first claim of radical value pluralism, Gray's case against classical liberalism would still be valid, if its second claim were true.

Gray acknowledges Berlin as his source for the view. Berlin in turn acknowledges Vico and Herder as his sources for it. The considerations which Berlin and Gray find in these writers are less than compelling.

Consider, first, the following representative passage from Berlin in which an attempt is made to argue for the view.

> Men, according to Herder, flourish only in congenial circumstances, that is, where the group to which they belong has achieved a fruitful relationship with the environment by which it is shaped and which in turn it shapes. . . . If Herder's view of mankind [is] correct . . . , and if each of the civilizations . . . are widely different, and indeed uncombinable – then how could there exist, even in principle, one universal ideal, valid for all men, at all times, everywhere? The 'physiognomies' of cultures are unique: each presents a wonderful exfoliation of human potentialities in its time and place and environment.[17]

The question which Berlin asks in this passage is rhetorical. It amounts to the claim that there cannot be a universal ideal valid for all men at all times. Berlin purports to be able to derive the claim from an insight he ascribes to Herder. The putative insight is that human beings can flourish only where the groups to which they belong have achieved some fruitful relationship with their environment resulting in some unique form of culture which represents some unique exfoliation of human potentialities. However, the conclusion simply does not follow from the premises. It might well be true that human beings can flourish only where the societies of which they are members have achieved some fruitful relationship with their environment in a way that has resulted in some unique culture. It does not follow from this that human beings can flourish only within those forms of culture which have developed within the groups of which they are members or within which they have been acculturated.

An analogy will help make this clear. It may well be true of plants that they can flourish only when the environment within which they are cultivated is congenial to them. It does not follow that there is only one environment within which plants belonging to any species can flourish! Moreover, different species of plants might well need different environments from one another to flourish. But it is conceivable that they could all be assembled together in some botanical garden and made to flourish in close proximity with one another. This could be done, provided the garden was arranged so that each different species be given a different micro-environment appropriate for it.

At this point, Berlin might wish to object that the analogy proves his point. All the different species of plants can be made to flourish within the imaginary botanical garden only by each being given a separate special micro-environment of their own. In contrast, human beings are members of one and the same society only if they share common institutions. It is these institutions which, in the case of human beings, are the analogue to the soil and climate in the case of plants. Consequently, if, as Berlin and Gray claim, human beings need different institutions from one another to flourish, as plants of different species need different climates within which to flourish, then human beings cannot all flourish within the same form of society as one another, as all different species of plant might be able to do within the same botanical garden.

However, this reply takes the botanical analogy too seriously. There are distinct limits to the range of natural environments within which each species of plant is capable of flourishing. These limits are such that there is no one natural environment within which all different species of plant are capable of flourishing together. However, the very indeterminacy of human nature and the artefactuality of human personality, to which Berlin and Gray attach such importance, make human beings very different from plants in this respect. The respective 'natural' environments within which all distinct peoples or nations flourish may not be able to coexist within the same form of society. This might be so, since these environments consist of institutions which may be incompatible with one another and with liberal institutions. It does not follow that there is no single form of society within which all distinct peoples are capable of flourishing alongside one another. This is so, notwithstanding the marked differences in the distinct forms of society which each of these peoples created for themselves when separate.

It is clear that, were one world civilization to replace the mass of separate cultures, then certain *forms of societal order* would die out. But if no one were to lose out by the convergence of all peoples in some such common culture, and if some were to gain, then the fact that there would disappear certain distinct forms of culture within which human beings had flourished need not be a net loss for anyone, let alone for everyone. Isaiah Berlin claims that, for people of one culture to appreciate the forms of flourishing made possible by another, it is necessary for them to have recourse to sympathetic imagination. In a world civilization from which certain forms of life had gone, people could still have access through this means to the cultural achievements of these vanished worlds.

Much the same lacuna can be found to undermine such argument as Gray offers for the second of the two claims of radical value pluralism. He writes

> Plural realism recognizes that, since the nature of human beings is a question for them, since it is only partly determinate and is therefore partly self-defined, no single conception of the good life can be founded

on a conception of human nature. This follows inexorably from the recognition that human beings, unlike other animal species, transform their needs and are part self-creators, over time and in history For this reason, on the plural realist view, no form of the good life can be final, any more than any can be said to be uniquely rational or natural.[18]

It is true that human beings do transform their needs over time. If for no other reason, they are in part self-creators. However, *pace* Gray, it does not follow that a single conception of the good life cannot be founded on a conception of human nature. Nor does it follow that some form of the good life cannot be said to be uniquely rational. More specifically, from the fact that human beings are in part self-creators, it cannot be inferred that it is not possible by means of an appeal to human nature to demonstrate that the liberal form of political association is best and uniquely rational for all human beings. For it might still nonetheless be true that, no matter the variety of human personality types, *everyone* would stand to benefit, in terms of the degree of happiness they could innocuously attain, through their society being or becoming liberal in form. This is so, even if its so doing would lead to the demise of certain traditional ways of life within which members of these societies had previously attained well-being. Thus, even if both constituent claims of radical value pluralism were true, it would not follow that the liberal polity was not best for all human beings. Given radical value pluralism, the liberal polity is other than best, only if there are certain forms of well-being available within illiberal societies that are not available within liberal regimes. This is an issue to which we shall return in section 5.7 below.

5.5 PERSONAL AUTONOMY AND WELL-BEING IN MODERN PLURALISTIC SOCIETY

As regards the well-being of members of present-day Western pluralistic societies, Gray advances two claims. The first is that for them to enjoy well-being, it is necessary that they possess personal autonomy. The second is that for them to be able to enjoy well-being, it is not sufficient that the polities of which they are members be liberal ones in the classical liberal sense. The measure of liberty which a liberal polity accords its members is deemed insufficient for their being able to enjoy well-being. It is claimed insufficient for two reasons. First, consider those who through disability, illness or lack of employment opportunity are permanently or temporarily unable to provide for themselves. In their case, the measure of liberty accorded them by a liberal polity will not suffice to ensure the satisfaction of all those basic needs which require satisfaction for them to enjoy well-being. Second, even in the case of those able to provide for themselves through their own efforts, the measure of liberty accorded by the liberal polity is unable to guarantee that their environment provides them with a sufficiently large range of choice-worthy options, without which personal autonomy cannot be exercised. To remedy the first of these defects of the liberal polity, Gray advocates what he calls *an enabling welfare-state*, and to overcome the second *a social market economy*.

Gray acknowledges Joseph Raz as the source of his view of the value and conditions of personal autonomy. Our object is to decide on the validity of this view of the value and conditions of autonomy for members of present-day pluralistic societies. We shall begin by examining the considerations offered by Raz and Gray in support of their claim that personal autonomy is an essential ingredient of the well-being of members of a modern pluralistic society. Because they offer somewhat different considerations from one another, we shall have to consider their views separately.

A striking feature of Raz's account of why personal autonomy is a vital ingredient of well-being is that the value it assigns to autonomy is instrumental. He writes as follows:

> For those who live in an autonomy-supporting environment there is no choice but to be autonomous: there is no other way to prosper in such a society. . . . The value of personal autonomy is a fact of life. Since we live in a society whose social forms are to a considerable extent based on individual choice, and since our options are limited by what is available in our society, we can prosper in it only if we can be successfully autonomous. . . . [U]ltimately those who live in an autonomy enhancing culture can prosper only by being autonomous.[19]

What reasons does Raz offer in support of his claim that modern Westerners need personal autonomy in order to prosper? His reasons are less than fully transparent but would seem to be as follows. Within modern societies, individuals are given personal choice over many aspects of their lives, such as career and marital partner. Members of traditional societies, typically, are denied much personal choice in these matters. Where members of a society are given personal choice in respect of them, then the character of these aspects of their lives becomes profoundly altered as a result. So altered do things like career, marriage and religion become in a society in which they are made matters of individual choice, that, in order for individuals to make a success of these matters, it is necessary for them to possess personal autonomy in respect of them. For example, if a person's career is to be decided by the individual in question, then, in order for the career on which someone embarks to be that in which that individual is most likely to succeed, their choice of career needs to be an autonomous choice. That is, the choice has to be made by the individual with a consciousness of what he or she is doing, from among worthwhile alternatives, and free from coercion and manipulation by others.

Raz is undoubtedly correct that, where matters are decided by individuals for themselves rather than determined for them by tradition, the character of these important aspects of their lives, such as marriage and career, does undergo a profound qualitative change. Raz is also undoubtedly correct that, where these aspects of their life are matters of individual choice, it is better for people that they make these choices autonomously. However, these facts do not by themselves establish that those who live within societies where these aspects of life are determined by their choice need personal autonomy in order to prosper. For it is possible that those individuals might be able to prosper still more, if those aspects of their lives were to be decided for them by tradition, rather than by individual choice. Were this so, then, presumably, such individuals would not need personal autonomy in order to prosper.

I am not intending to deny that people are better-off where they can decide these aspects of life for themselves. Nor am I wishing to dispute Raz's claim that, where they can and must decide these aspects of their lives for themselves, individuals need personal autonomy in order to prosper. However, before it is possible to show that personal autonomy is an essential ingredient of personal well-being of people who are at liberty to decide these matters for themselves, something else must *first* be established. This is that people are better-off by having to decide these aspects of lives for themselves, rather than having them decided by tradition. Therefore, in order for Raz to establish that members of modern pluralistic cultures need personal autonomy in order to prosper, he must provide an argument which he conspicuously fails to do. This is an argument to show that people are better-off when, instead of tradition deciding their careers, marital partners and religions, they are accorded the liberty to decide these aspects of their individual lives for themselves.

An analogy may help make this clear. Suppose I claim that you need to diet and I am asked why. Suppose I reply that only by so doing can you lose weight. What I cite in support of my initial claim may well be true. But I will not thereby have justified my claim that you need to diet, unless I can establish that you need to lose weight. Similarly, Raz claims that members of modern pluralistic societies need personal autonomy to prosper. He then attempts to substantiate this claim by citing in support of it the fact that only by their having personal autonomy can individuals succeed in those aspects of their lives which modern pluralistic societies make matters of personal decision. This fact, however, shows that such individuals need personal autonomy, only if something else is also true of them. This is that such individuals are better-off through having personal liberty to decide these matters of their lives than they would be were such matters decided for members of their society by tradition. This is something for which Raz offers no argument. Consequently, he has offered no real argument on behalf of his claim that personal autonomy is an ingredient of well-being of members of modern pluralistic societies.

Does Gray do any better than Raz in establishing the case for personal autonomy? Again, he does not. The considerations which Gray adduces in support of his claim that personal autonomy is a vital ingredient of the well-being of moderns are no less question-begging than Raz's. Thus, on one occasion, Gray writes

> The claim being made here is not that autonomy is a universal good, but that it is an essential element in any good life that can be lived *by us*. No inhabitant of a modern pluralistic, mobile and discursive society can fare well without at least a modicum of the capacities and resources needed for autonomy. . . . Autonomy is not a necessary element in human flourishing *tout court*. It is an essential element of the good life for people situated in our historical context as inheritors of a particular, individualist form of life.[20]

Only upon one further supposition does this argument succeed in showing autonomy to be an essential ingredient of the well-being of members of modern pluralistic societies. This is that their well-being depends upon these aspects of their lives being matters of their personal choice. However, when arguing for *this* latter thesis, Gray appeals to the contribution to their personal autonomy that is made when these aspects of their lives are made matters of their individual choice! He writes

> The value of negative liberty . . . must be theorized in terms of its contribution to something other than itself, which does possess intrinsic value. In truth, it seems clear that the chief value of negative liberty is in its contribution to the positive liberty of autonomy. . . . The ethical standing of the market is its status as a necessary condition of one vital ingredient of human well-being, individual autonomy.[21]

Now, people are members of modern, discursive societies only in virtue of their society according them negative liberties of one form or another.

These include such liberties as those of thought and expression, freedom of contract, and so on. Gray argues for these negative liberties on the grounds that they promote the personal autonomy of those to whom these liberties are accorded. However, this does nothing to show that these liberties are essential to the well-being of those accorded them. For the only justification Gray has so far offered for his claim that such people need personal autonomy in order to attain well-being is that personal autonomy enables them to choose well in the presence of these negative liberties!

Elsewhere, Gray does offer an additional argument on behalf of the value of autonomy. He writes

> Among us – the inhabitants of modern Western societies characterized by a high degree of social mobility, pluralism in lifestyles and individualism in ethical culture – autonomy is a constitutive ingredient in any form of the good life. If we lacked even a modicum of autonomy, if we were not even part authors of our lives – if our jobs, our marriages or sexual partners, our place of abode or our religion were assigned to us or chosen for us – we would consider our individuality stifled and the goodness of our lives diminished.[22]

This amounts to a second argument for the claim that autonomy is a vital ingredient of the well-being of members of modern pluralistic society. The grounds now are that such people value being able to express their individuality. But there is a gap in the argument. For Gray to establish that possession of personal autonomy is an essential ingredient of the well-being of members of modern pluralistic societies, it is not enough for him to cite the fact that people growing up in such societies would feel themselves deprived of an essential ingredient of their well-being, if denied personal autonomy. These people might be mistaken in thinking that personal autonomy is an essential ingredient of their well-being. What Gray needs to provide is some argument which establishes that people growing up in these societies would have been deprived of a vital ingredient of well-being were their societies not to provide them with personal autonomy. That these people believe they need personal autonomy does not make that belief correct.

What Gray needs to be able to show is that, for some reason other than the fact that they value having it, those who value being able to express their individuality are able to lead better lives when they have it than when they do not. Their valuing being able to lead such lives cannot itself be the source of such lives being better. And, he needs to show that these autonomous lives would be better for these people, quite apart from appealing to the fact that they value what makes such lives possible. For precisely what is at issue is whether their having what makes such autonomous lives possible for them – namely, the negative liberties – does, indeed, make their lives better than they would be without these liberties.

The outcome of our examination of their arguments for the value of personal autonomy is this. Neither Raz nor Gray provides any convincing and non-question-begging argument in support of their claim that personal autonomy is an essential ingredient of the well-being of members of modern pluralistic society. This does not mean that personal autonomy does not have this status. It only means we have yet to be shown that it does.

Let us, then, consider, independently of Gray or Raz, whether personal autonomy has such a status. As Raz and Gray construe personal autonomy, someone possesses it if and only if that person possesses three things: first, appropriate mental abilities, notably the capacity to form sufficiently complex and long-term intentions as to be able to make and execute plans; second, the awareness of a large range of worthwhile options from which to choose; and, third, the liberty to choose from among these options.

It certainly would appear that, if all three conditions are satisfied by someone, that person has all he or she needs for personal well-being. Or, at least, it would seem that, if, in such circumstances, an individual fails to attain well-being, that individual has no one but themselves to blame for not doing so. However, to justify the claim that personal autonomy is a *vital* ingredient of the well-being of members of modern pluralistic societies, what has to be shown is not that they *can* attain well-being when they enjoy personal autonomy. Rather, what must be shown is that they cannot attain well-being *without* enjoying personal autonomy. This is an entirely different matter.

There is one condition of personal autonomy, as Gray and Raz understand the notion, which it seems impossible to establish is a necessary ingredient of the well-being of an individual. This is the individual's *having a large range of worthwhile options from which to choose*. Suppose someone only has one. Why should having such a small range of options preclude well-being? To see this, suppose someone lives in a modern, pluralistic society. Suppose further that he or she had been brought up to be a devout practitioner of a faith, such that the pattern of their life is so rigidly and thoroughly prescribed for them that effectively, in their eyes, there is only one way in which they can live. No other way of living has any value for them. Suppose, that the life that they consider rigidly prescribed for them is not itself unworthy of choice. Say, the way of living they believe demanded of them is one which demands probity, hard-work, fidelity, beneficence, and so on of them. The individual in question could not be thought of as possessing personal autonomy, according to Raz's and Gray's definition of it. This is because the beliefs of that individual would leave that individual without a range of worthwhile options from which to choose. It might be argued that these beliefs would not leave the individual without such a range of options. For, it might be claimed, the individual could always break out of his or her belief-system. However, were this argued, it becomes hard to see how, given the beliefs of the individual, having this range of options is *necessary* for their well-being. Would such people lack any vital ingredient of well-being, if they lived in the only way they considered worthwhile? I cannot see how they could be thought to do so.

It follows that there is only one set of people in modern pluralistic societies for whose well-being the possession of personal autonomy can be thought to be an essential ingredient. These are those who do not subscribe to any systems of belief which rigidly prescribe for them ways of living which are not unworthy of choice. There are plenty of such people about in modern pluralistic societies. But is there any reason to suppose it essential for their well-being that they possess personal autonomy? There would appear to be a sound reason. But it is a reason that does not appear to be given by Raz or Gray. We know that there are great differences between individuals in matters of temperament and taste. In the absence of belief systems which rigidly prescribe what individuals should do, given these differences between them, the chances of an individual being likely to attain well-being will be increased by their enjoying autonomy. For their possession of autonomy is likely to increase their chances of discovering which way of living their life most suits their own individual taste and temperament. Hence, for people who are without attachment to belief-systems which prescribe for them a way of life, but who must construct one from their own choices, it would appear that personal autonomy is an essential ingredient of their well-being. Since it is difficult for members of modern pluralistic society to retain allegiance to traditional belief-systems which prescribe their course of life for them, Raz and Gray are correct in maintaining personal autonomy to be a vital ingredient of the well-being of members of modern pluralistic societies.

Two further questions remain for us to consider before we can pronounce on the validity of Gray's critique of classical liberalism. The first is whether, as Gray contends, in order for members of a modern pluralistic society to be able to exercise personal autonomy, it is not sufficient, though it is necessary, that their society be liberal in form. More specifically, is Gray correct that, in order for members of such societies to enjoy sufficient personal autonomy to enable them to attain well-being, it is necessary that their polity incorporate a social market economy with an enabling welfare state, rather than merely being liberal according to the classical liberal conception? The second is whether, as Gray contends, in the case of the well-being of those who are not members of modern pluralistic societies, not only is such a form of polity not necessary for their well-being, it is necessary that their polity not be liberal in form. The first of these questions will be considered in the next section, the second in the one after that.

5.6   THE CONDITIONS OF PERSONAL AUTONOMY

Assume that members of a modern pluralistic society need to possess personal autonomy to attain well-being. What do they need in order to possess personal autonomy? Is it sufficient that they possess that measure of liberty accorded by a liberal polity? Or is it additionally necessary that their polity be a social market economy with an enabling welfare state? According to Gray, it is the latter.

A *social market economy* is a form of market society supplemented by a range of state-financed institutions designed to promote the well-being of members of society in ways the market is supposedly unable to do. Gray argues that, unless its market economy is so supplemented, few members of modern pluralistic societies can be assured of sufficient personal autonomy for their attainment of well-being. He claims this, notwithstanding the measure of liberty accorded them within such a polity, and even if they are not in need of any state welfare.

The vital ingredient of worthwhile autonomy which Gray says that people cannot be guaranteed by the market, and which the state has, therefore, to supply, is a cultural environment rich in worthwhile options and amenities. Without such an environment, individuals may have all the mental capacities to make autonomous choices, as well as the liberty and power to act upon them. However, they will no more be capable of personal autonomy than will a man trapped in a pit who possesses an adequate food-supply but who cannot escape.

According to Gray, a cultural environment is sufficiently well-stocked with choice-worthy options and amenities when and only when its members are able, if they wish, to enjoy, as participants or spectators, such forms of high culture as opera, pure research, and deep romantic attachments and familial bonds. Unless provision of such options is made the deliberate object of government policy in the form of such things as state subsidy for the arts and pure sciences, then such an environment cannot be guaranteed to members of society and their well-being is prejudiced.

Much the same is argued by Gray in the case of what he calls *an enabling welfare state*. Without one, some members of a modern pluralistic society will not be able to enjoy worthwhile personal autonomy. This is because their basic needs will, or may, go unsatisfied. *A basic need*, we are told, is 'one whose satisfaction is essential to the possibility of a worthwhile life, and whose frustration makes impossible the living of a good life. . . . Basic needs encompass need whose satisfaction contributes to, or enhances autonomy, such as needs for food, housing, medical care, education, and so forth.'[23]

Gray's view is that, without an enabling welfare state, the basic needs of many would go untended in a modern pluralistic society. Those whose basic needs would go unsatisfied would be the sick, the disabled, and those who, though able-bodied and competent, are unable to find employment. The basic needs of all these unfortunates can be satisfied only by forms of state welfare that encompass support, retraining and education. In the case of the sick and disabled, the state must provide health care and other benefits sufficient to enable them 'to lead a life that is as autonomous, as dignified and as meaningful as that of the able-bodied'.[24] It is, thus, with perfect accuracy that Gray observes that '[t]he functions I have ascribed to government, and the range of policies that I have argued come under its responsibility, are far larger than anything acceptable to . . . a classical liberal perspective . . .'.[25]

How persuasive is Gray's argument that the measure of liberty accorded members of a liberal polity is insufficient for the enjoyment by them of as much personal autonomy as they need for well-being? How compelling are his reasons for claiming that it needs to be augmented by a social market and an enabling welfare state?

Gray's strictures against the sufficiency of the liberal polity for the well-being of its members are vulnerable on several counts.[26] First, it may readily be conceded to Gray that someone can possess a sufficient degree of personal autonomy for the attainment of well-being only if there is some choice-worthy option available which that person has the ability to identify as worthy of choice, and choose. However, it need not be conceded that, for such options to be available to all members of a polity, anything more is needed than that measure of liberty accorded by a liberal polity. Having available a large array of choice-worthy options from which to choose might make it easier for someone to attain well-being through exercising personal autonomy. It is by no means necessary for a person to have such a large array of choice-worthy options in order to have sufficient for well-being. As Chandran Kukathas has observed, even a slave can possess enough choice-worthy options to be able to exercise sufficient personal autonomy for the attainment of well-being. Obviously, the fewer the choice-worthy options available to a person, the harder it is for that person to attain well-being by the exercise of personal autonomy. But, so long as there is at least one such option, it is possible for a person to attain well-being through exercising personal autonomy. In this vital respect, the situation of members of a liberal polity is not akin to that of someone trapped in a pit with enough food to live on.

It follows, therefore, that whether a liberal polity is better able than a social market economy with an enabling welfare state to promote the well-being of its members turns on the following question. Which of these two societal forms is better at promoting the personal autonomy of its members? *Pace* Gray, there are very good reasons for supposing that it is the liberal polity. As Kukathas has also observed, personal autonomy is a matter of character and resolution. Although ostensibly designed to augment the choice-worthy options available to members of society, an enabling welfare state and social market economy are all too liable to foster forms of dependency that sap resolution and determination. The history of state-welfare in the USA and Britain does not inspire confidence in the ability of the sort of state recommended by Gray to promote its members' autonomy. Rather, it has been a tale of ever-greater dependency and a diminution in personal responsibility.

Further, it is highly doubtful whether government is better than civil society at providing its citizens with a cultural environment rich in choice-worthy options. This is so for two reasons. First, state institutions designed to promote and safeguard culture are all too easily subject to being taken over by interest groups who substitute some agenda of their own. Consider, for example, the damage that has been done to the curriculum in secondary and higher education, when it becomes a matter for the state. Again, consider the ease with which it has become possible for very dubious activities to have been able to receive state subsidy in the form of grants.

Additionally, where the state includes as part of its agenda the subsidy of such forms of activity as opera and pure research, it becomes all too easy for it to acquire a degree of control over those activities that presages ill for them. Personal autonomy is not likely to be much enhanced when it is the state, rather than a plurality of independent individuals and private bodies, that decides what forms of artistic endeavour and research are worthy of support. For these reasons, therefore, we may be sceptical of Gray's claim that the personal autonomy of members of modern pluralistic societies is better promoted by a form of polity that incorporates a social market economy with an enabling welfare state than it is by the liberal polity advocated by classical liberals.

It only remains for us now to consider whether Gray is correct in claiming, of those who have not been acculturated within modern pluralistic societies, that liberal political institutions are not only not necessary for their well-being, but can and are likely to be positively inimical to it.

5.7 HUMAN WELL-BEING AND ILLIBERAL SOCIETY

It will be recalled that radical value pluralism comprised two claims. The first is that there exists such a variety of uncombinable and incommensurable human goods that there is no single form of human well-being best for everyone. The second is that human nature is so indeterminate and human personality so artefactual that human beings are only capable of attaining those forms of well-being which are possible within the forms of society in which they have been acculturated.

Our discussion of radical value pluralism led us to the following interim conclusion. Even if the theory were correct in both its claims, it would not follow that those who have not been acculturated within liberal regimes could not benefit from their societies becoming liberal. It would follow that they could not do so, only if, besides radical value pluralism, something else were also true. This is that there are certain forms of human well-being which are possible only within non-liberal societies.

It is evident that it is upon some such thesis as this that Gray is relying in much of what he writes about human well-being within illiberal societies. Consider, for example, the following observations.

> Who can doubt that human beings flourished under the feudal institutions of medieval Christendom? Or under the monarchical government of medieval Christendom?[27]

> It is evident . . . that there are many forms of human flourishing that cannot coexist with liberal equality. All excellences that depend upon inherited hierarchy or involuntary subordination, that presuppose the embeddedness of persons in roles and statuses that are constitutive of their identities and from which they are unfree to exit.[28]

> There are many forms of human flourishing that depend upon inequalities that any liberal view must reject.[29]

> Recognition of a pluralism of forms of human flourishing, each objective, of which only some can exist in a liberal regime, destroys the authority of liberalism as a universal, trans-historical and cross-cultural ideal.[30]

Illiberal societies said by Gray to be capable of harbouring forms of human flourishing not obtainable within liberal regimes include the authoritarian civil societies of modern East Asia – South Korea, Taiwan, and Hong Kong.[31] Gray writes

> The Western, and especially the American, project of forcing liberalization on Japanese economic life, though it is bound to fail, is thoroughly and dangerously misconceived. It neglects the embeddedness of economic transactions in an underlying culture that is not, and is most unlikely to become, individualist. In both Russia and Japan, Westernization (or further Westernization) would only involve injury to valuable social forms, with few, if any, corresponding advantages.[32]

In addition to these present-day illiberal societies, Gray considers that certain hierarchical and authoritarian forms of order within medieval feudal society made possible forms of well-being with which liberal institutions are deemed incompatible. Thus, he writes that '[m]any virtues are weak or absent from liberal society: for example the virtues of a courtier or of a pious peasant presuppose a social order that cannot coexist with the liberal society.'[33]

Is Gray correct that there are distinct forms of well-being and excellence that are available only to members of hierarchical and authoritarian forms of society? I cannot see that anything he has said shows there are. It is true that no one can be a courtier without a court or a bushido warrior in a liberal society. But this only shows that a certain *way* of achieving well-being in an illiberal society would not be possible in a liberal society. It does not show that the form of well-being made possible by that historical way of life would not still be possible through living in some other way were that illiberal form of society to have become liberal. For example, being a bushido warrior is a way of achieving that form of well-being associated with the possession of honour, physical prowess, loyalty, fitness and so on. All these qualities are surely possible without having to be a bushido warrior. Suppose the artefactuality of human personality means that human beings are unable to enjoy any forms of well-being other than those possible within the societies within which they have been acculturated. It still might be true, as classical liberalism claims, that every human being would be better-off were their society liberal. For there might be no form of well-being possible in an illiberal society that is not also possible in a liberal society. I deny that radical value pluralism establishes that there are any such forms of well-being. On the question whether members of illiberal societies stand to benefit or lose from their societies becoming liberal, the only relevant consideration is whether they would be better-off in terms of well-being were their societies to become liberal. Nothing in value pluralism suggests otherwise.

Further, an unbiased consideration of illiberal societies suggests that, were their societies to have become liberal, their members would benefit in terms of their own conception of well-being. So far as medieval society is concerned, the following comment of Nathaniel Branden seems eminently sound.

> The complete lack of control over any aspect of one's existence, the ruthless suppression of intellectual freedom, the paralysing restrictions on any form of individual initiative and independence . . . are cardinal characteristics of the Middle Ages . . . along with the famines, the plagues, the exhausting labour from sunrise to sunset, the suffocating routine, the superstitious terror, the attacks of mass hysteria afflicting entire towns, the nightmare brutality of men's dealings with one another, [and] the use of legalized torture as a normal way of life. . . . In pre-capitalist centuries, . . . an unconscionable amount of labour was required to make or acquire the simplest necessities – and the general standard of living was appallingly low; human existence was a continual, exhausting struggle against imminent starvation. About half of the children born, perished before the age of ten.[34]

This leaves contemporary East Asian societies cited by Gray as a counter-example to the universalist claims of classical liberalism. There is little reason for thinking that, ultimately, anyone within them is better-off as a result of such illiberal characteristics as they retain. Consider present-day Japan, for example. Its population, as well as arguably everyone else, are arguably much the worse for its lack of liberal institutions. For example, because it prohibits the importation of rice which is Japan's staple food, there is an acute shortage of land as well as vastly inflated food prices. Land shortages cause property prices to be extremely high and thereby condemn ordinary Japanese to live in very cramped accommodation. The following recent account of Japanese society suggests that, *pace* Gray, it will not be possible for much longer for Japan to retain for much longer its traditional values and illiberal trade policies.

> Japanese society is increasingly split between landowners and the rest. . . . The new magnates of finance and speculation are, broadly speaking, resented by the average Japanese. . . . The descendants of samurai warriors, inheritors of an ascetic tradition, have been astonishingly quick to adapt to the new consumerism of moisturizing creams and designer fashions. . . . Japanese society is . . . making a headlong dash to consume

that threatens to erode its traditional values. . . . The 'silent majority' of Japanese are increasingly ill-disposed to accept without question the traditional pattern of life shaped by work, thrift, and civic duty.

The Japanese economy cannot escape the consequences of this galloping Americanization of its culture, and notably of its young people. The snob value automatically attached to foreign luxury goods . . . could undermine the habit of saving . . . one of the great strengths of the Japanese economy.

As they gradually acquire a taste for hedonism and mass consumerism, Japanese workers are likely to develop a corresponding detachment from the work ethic and their traditional devotion to the company.[35]

Our examination of Gray's arguments against classical liberalism allow us to conclude that Gray has not provided any convincing reasons for supposing that a liberal polity is not in the best interests of all human beings, regardless of the forms of society within which they have been acculturated. It is only where someone's interests have not been rightly understood that it can appear to be otherwise. This completes my review of all the main contemporary forms of opposition to classical liberalism. None has proved compelling. The liberal polity remains an unvanquished ideal.

6 Conclusion

For anyone to espouse classical liberalism today is almost certainly for them to run the risk of being accused of intellectual naivety or, still worse, moral corruption. 'How can anyone favour a form of political order today that has proved to be so manifestly at variance with the interests of the majority of its members? Its present-day support can only come from a rich selfish minority whose interests it does favour, together with whichever unscrupulous intellectuals the rich can hire to produce propaganda on their behalf, plus whoever is gullible enough to be taken in by it. Anyone favouring this form of order today, therefore, must be oblivious of or insensitive to its baneful effects on the life-prospects of the vast majority. Those espousing classical liberalism today, therefore, are deficient either in intellectual sense or moral sensibility, or in both respects.'

The preceding chapters have examined the warrant for this accusation. In all, against the form of societal order championed by classical liberalism, its present-day critics level three charges. Modern liberals find morally unconscionable the inequality it permits. Communitarians find its individualism corrosive of community and ethical life. Modern conservatives claim the cultural pluralism it tolerates corrosive of allegiance, and its minimal government unable to satisfy the basic needs of its members without doing which it justifiably lacks legitimacy in their eyes.

These charges have been examined in the preceding chapters and found lacking in substance. The life-prospects of society's less well-off members are not likely to improve if and when redistributive political institutions replace those which generate the inequalities which modern egalitarian liberals find so unconscionable. Such egalitarian reforms are only likely to discourage the formation of capital and encourage its dissipation. Since it is upon the formation of capital that the continued and enhanced well-being of members ultimately depends, redistributive measures and institutions favoured by modern liberals are ultimately unlikely to benefit those whom they are ostensibly designed to benefit.

Within the liberal form of order, the comparatively well-off do not enjoy their greater wealth and opportunity at the expense of the less well-off. Were people not at liberty to acquire and enjoy secure possession of the greater wealth than others, it is unlikely such wealth would be brought into existence at all and hence be available for redistribution. It is unlikely, therefore, that, in the long term, the comparatively less well-off would enjoy any long-term improvement in their life-prospects were society's wealth distributed equally to all and all further inequality prohibited from arising.

No doubt, as many modern egalitarian liberals are at pains to emphasize, there is an important sense in which everyone is equally deserving of moral concern and consideration. However, that they are does not in itself morally dictate that they should enjoy equality of wealth and opportunity. It only dictates that, in considering which form of societal order is best, everyone's well-being be taken equally into account. If, as classical liberals maintain, everyone is likely to be better-off within a liberal form of order than within any other, there is no reason for thinking that considerations of impartiality and the equal moral status of all human beings dictate any more egalitarian form of order than that.

As regards the communitarian charge, no reason was found for supposing that the measure of individualism which the liberal order sanctions is so great as to preclude community or as rich and full an ethical life as anyone might desire. The form of order endorsed by classical liberalism compels all members of society to display a minimal concern for one another by legally requiring them to refrain from harming one another. This renders the society a minimal form of community at least. Additionally, through providing maximum scope and incentive for mutually advantageous voluntary exchange, this form of order further encourages among its members both interdependence and positive service to one another.

Outside the sphere of the market, enormous scope remains within a liberal order for the closer bonds of association characteristic of closer forms of community. The liberal order is perfectly compatible with a whole plethora of forms of communal association to which individuals can belong. These range from family, through church and voluntary charitable organizations, to participating in political life, even merely in the capacity of voting. It is false that the pursuit of wealth is or must be subversive of virtues like honesty and justice or that it undermines traditional forms of life for which other virtues are necessary. Moreover, there is no good reason to suppose that their own personal happiness – which, of necessity, includes that of their loved ones – does not provide individual members of a liberal societal order with a *telos* sufficiently determinate in form as to provide a rationale for the acquisition and exercise by them of all the traditional virtues.

Again, contrary to what its conservative critics maintain, there is nothing about the liberal form of societal order that undermines in its members either allegiance or a sense of its legitimacy. Genuinely liberal societies would, indeed, be open to and liable to attract immigrants of different ethnic and cultural background to those of the majority of the indigenous population. However, there is no reason for thinking that a liberal form of order must be unable to forge and preserve a common national identity among all its members sufficient for their common allegiance. Nor was any good reason found to suppose the liberal form of order unable to satisfy the basic needs of all members, including that for an environment rich in goods of culture. Nor, finally, did we find any good reason to doubt that members of illiberal societies would not too ultimately benefit through their societies becoming liberal, irrespective of what in the way of tradition might have to be sacrificed in the process.

No classical liberal is so starry-eyed as to suggest that a utopia is or will ever be possible in which all human problems have been solved and complete happiness and virtue attained by every member. However, on behalf of their preferred form of societal order, a no less important, if somewhat less extravagant, claim has been defended in this work. This is that *this form of order enables its members to attain greater well-being or happiness than does any other societal form.*

There would appear to be only two possible ways to resist this conclusion. The first is to deny that forms of societal order should be appraised by reference to the degree to which they promote the well-being of their members. The second is to deny that the liberal form of societal order is that which best enables human beings to attain happiness.

There appears little to commend the first possible line of resistance. How else can or should different societal forms of order be appraised other than in terms of the extent to which they enable their members to enjoy as much happiness or well-being as possible? Such a benchmark would certainly appear to be common ground to both classical liberals and many of those contemporary critics of classical liberalism considered here.

So far as the second possible line of resistance is concerned, this seems, of all the many ways of resisting classical liberalism, the one on which the unpersuaded are most likely to fasten. For, it will be said, it is simply incredible that a form of order which makes so little statutory provision for the welfare of society's unfortunates can be recommended on the grounds that it better promotes their well-being than do other societal forms. 'Take a look around at the poverty, squalor, and degradation that afflicts any large Western metropolis today and you will see just how implausible it is to suppose that a liberal order, which would stop all state welfare and legalise drugs and prostitution, offers society's less fortunate members the best possible lives of which they are capable.'

It must be admitted straightaway that anyone venturing today on to the streets of any large Western metropolis, particularly in their less savoury areas, can hardly fail to be aware of enormous amounts of squalor, poverty and degradation within them. Down-and-outs, drunks, drug-addicts, prostitutes and the homeless are all too conspicuous in major cities throughout Western Europe and North America. Equally, a casual glance at any of their national daily newspapers will reveal massive levels of crime of the most gruesome sort, particularly violent crime of all forms and theft. Opponents of classical liberalism regard the disturbingly high levels of vice, crime and squalor so prevalent in contemporary Western societies to establish that classical liberalism must be mistaken as to which form of societal order is best for all its members. For these critics construe these insalubrious features of contemporary life to be the result of attempts by recent conservative governments to pursue a classical liberal agenda and cut back public expenditure, or else, regard these social problems as eradicable only by various forms of state activity, ranging from more extensive welfare to job-creation schemes, and the like, which no classical liberal could sanction.

There is, however, good reason to reject these anti-classical liberal explanations of and prescribed remedies for these social ills. There is reason for thinking that these social ills exist on as large a scale as they do today, less because of the extent to which these societies conform to classical liberal principles, than because of the extent to which they do not. This can be argued on the basis of three effects which the massive growth of state welfare has had this century. The first is a decline in private philanthropy. The second is the destruction of the capacity of most individuals to provide for themselves and their dependants those goods and services, such as housing, education and health care, which the welfare state has undertaken to provide everyone. The third is the massive rise in crime since the 1960s.

So far as the first of these effects is concerned, there is statistical evidence to suggest that private philanthropy is inversely proportional to the size of public provision of welfare.[1] The relevance of this fact becomes apparent when taken in conjunction with the other displacement effect of the rise of the welfare state already mentioned. This is its having prevented most ordinary able-bodied people from being able and willing to supply for themselves and without need of state assistance those goods which the welfare state provides. It has become apparent from a comparatively recent body of historiographical research that, prior to the creation of the welfare state, most individuals provided through their own resources for themselves and their dependants those goods and services which the welfare state does.[2] This holds true for education, housing, medical insurance and pensions. There is no reason to suppose that most people would not have continued to make private provision had the rise of the welfare state not relieved them of the need – and, more importantly, the means – to do so.

When these two effects of the rise of the welfare state are taken together, they suggest that those unable to provide for themselves and genuinely in need of assistance need not necessarily be net beneficiaries of the system of state welfare. For it is arguable that they might have received better provision through self-help and private philanthropic endeavour had the welfare state not developed.

Likewise, the growth of the welfare state has arguably been a major factor in the recent and disturbing massive rise of crime. Critics of classical liberalism tend to attribute such crime to deprivation, poverty and lack of job opportunities. However, this diagnosis seems dubious, since crime rates were lower during preceding periods in which these alleged causes of crime were far more severe.[3] It would thus seem that the current high levels of crime must be attributed to something else. One major social change which seems a likely explanation of the growth of crime has been the collapse of the two-parent family among the least well-educated and skilled members of the developed societies.[4] For the breakdown of the family among them on the scale which has occurred will have led young males from such backgrounds, who are responsible for a disproportionate amount of crime, to grow up in environments scarce in adult male role-models of responsible providers. Without the presence of such influential character-forming figures with whom they can identify, the likelihood that they will be drawn into criminal activity is arguably much higher than it would otherwise be.

One major factor responsible for the collapse of the two-parent family among such social classes has undoubtedly been the growth of state welfare. For it has enabled young women, without any appreciable reduction in living standards, to have and raise children without needing to be maintained by the fathers of these children. The rise of the welfare state would appear to have removed previously powerful economic disincentives for their doing so, and as a result created an environment conducive to criminality.

Suppose, as has been argued, that the recent increase in crime is directly attributable to the collapse of the two-parent family among the least skilled and educated sectors of the population. And, further suppose, as has also been argued, that this collapse is in turn directly attributable to the growth of the welfare state. It must, then, be that what has made and will continue to make the lives of so many people today less good than they might otherwise be is the extent to which their societies fail to exemplify, rather than exemplify, a classical liberal form.

So cultivated within statist assumptions has the late-twentieth-century political imagination become that it takes considerable effort to see classical liberal diagnoses of and prescriptions for dealing with today's social problems for what they are. They are not cynical or self-satisfied evasions of responsibility on the part of those who happen to be graced with good fortune. Rather, they are rather serious, well-intentioned, and, above all, well-founded prescriptions, based upon hard evidence and dispassionate reasoning.

No one who has fought themselves free of the intellectual stranglehold which anti-classical liberal political sentiment currently enjoys among intellectuals and opinion-formers can have any illusions about just how difficult the task will be to convince public opinion that the best solution to the manifold problems that afflict the world today is that recommended by classical liberalism. Equally, however, no one who has come to embrace classical liberalism will fail to appreciate that nothing less than its eventual triumph will enable human beings to enjoy the best lives of which they are capable. To this extent, classical liberals need have no embarrassment about being considered utopian in political aspiration. Unlike other forms of utopianism, the classical liberal variety springs less from naivety about what is humanly possible than from a suitably modest and realistic assessment about what would make human lives as good as they can be.

Notes

2 CLASSICAL LIBERALISM

1. Plato, *Republic*, 420b–421c passim, trans. D. Lee, Second Edition (Harmondsworth: Penguin, 1974), pp. 185–7 passim.
2. Aristotle, *Politics*, Book III, ch. 6, 1278 15–25, in *Basic Works of Aristotle*, ed. R. McKeon (New York: Random House, 1941), p. 1184.
3. Thomas Hobbes, *Leviathan*, ed. C. B. Macpherson (Harmondsworth: Penguin, 1968), p. 376.
4. John Locke, *Two Treatises of Government*, ed. P. Laslett, (Cambridge: Cambridge University Press, 1960), Second Treatise, sec. 90.
5. Ibid., sec. 95.
6. Ibid., sec. 142.
7. Adam Smith, *The Theory of Moral Sentiments* (Indianapolis: Liberty Classics, 1976), p. 305.
8. Adam Ferguson, *An Essay on the History of Civil Society*, ed. D. Forbes (Edinburgh: Edinburgh University Press, 1966), p. 58.
9. Henry Sidgwick, *The Elements of Politics* (London: Macmillan, 1891), p. 34.
10. Adam Smith, *The Wealth of Nations*, vol. 2, eds R. H. Campbell and A. S. Skinner (Shadeland, Indianapolis: Liberty Press, 1979), p. 687.
11. Ibid., pp. 687–8.
12. I derive this terminology from Lord Robbins, *Theory of Economic Policy in English Classical Political Economy*, Second Edition (London: Macmillan, 1978), pp. 186–93.
13. Robert Nozick, *Anarchy, State and Utopia* (New York: Basic Books, 1974) and David Gauthier, *Morals by Agreement* (Oxford: Clarendon Press, 1986).
14. Franz Brentano, *The Foundation and Construction of Ethics* (London: Routledge and Kegan Paul, 1973).
15. Ludwig von Mises, *Liberalism* (San Franscisco: Cobden Press, 1985), p. 10.
16. See John Emerich Edward Dalberg-Acton, 'The History of Freedom in Christianity', in Lord Acton, *Essays in the History of Liberty*, ed. J. R. Fears (Indianapolis: Liberty Press, 1986).

3 MODERN LIBERALISM

1. John Rawls, *A Theory of Justice* (Oxford: Clarendon Press, 1972).
2. Ibid., p. 4.
3. Ibid., p. 7.
4. Ibid., p. 7.
5. John Rawls, 'Justice as Fairness: Political not Metaphysical', *Philosophy and Public Affairs*, 1985, vol. 14, p. 227.
6. *A Theory of Justice*, p. 72.
7. Ibid., p. 72.

8. Ibid., p. 73.
9. Ibid., pp. 73–4.
10. Ibid., p. 74.
11. Ibid., p. 74.
12. Ibid., p. 102.
13. Ibid., p. 102.
14. I owe the criticisms that follow to David Gauthier, 'Justice and Natural Endowment: Toward a Critique of Rawls' Ideological Framework', *Social Theory and Practice*, vol. 3, 1974, pp. 3–26.
15. John Rawls, *Political Liberalism* (New York: Columbia University Press, 1993), pp. 276–7.
16. *A Theory of Justice*, p. 278.
17. David Gauthier, *Morals by Agreement* (Oxford: Clarendon Press, 1986), pp. 253–4.
18. Thomas Nagel, *Equality and Partiality* (New York: Oxford University Press, 1991).
19. Ibid., p. 35.
20. Ibid., pp. 38–9.
21. Ibid., pp. 81–2.
22. Ibid., pp. 65–8.
23. Ibid., p. 58.
24. Ibid., p. 64.
25. Ronald Dworkin, 'What is Equality?' in two parts: Part 1, Equality of Welfare, *Philosophy and Public Affairs* (Summer 1981); Part II, Equality of Resources, *Philosophy and Public Affairs* (Fall 1981); 'Why Liberals Should Believe in Equality', *New York Review of Books* (3 February 1983), pp. 32–4; 'In Defence of Equality', in *Social Philosophy and Policy*, vol. 1, issue 1 (Autumn 1983), pp. 24–40.
26. R. Dworkin, 'Why Liberals Should Believe in Equality', *New York Review of Books*, 3 February 1983, pp. 32–4, 33.
27. Ibid., p. 32.
28. Ibid., p. 32.
29. R. Dworkin, 'Liberalism', in S. Hampshire (ed.), *Public and Private Morality* (Cambridge: Cambridge University Press, 1978), p. 127.
30. Kai Nielsen, *Equality and Liberty: A Defence of Radical Egalitarianism* (Totowa, New Jersey: Rowman and Allanheld Publishers, 1985).
31. Ibid., pp. 7–8.
32. Ibid., pp. 288–9.
33. Ibid., p. 7.
34. Ted Honderich, *Conservatism* (London: Hamish Hamilton, 1990).
35. Ibid., pp. 234–5.
36. Ibid., p. 60.
37. F. A. Hayek, *Individualism and the Economic Order* (Chicago: University of Chicago Press, 1948), p. 14.
38. *Conservatism*, p. 73.
39. Franz Brentano, *The Foundation and Construction of Ethics* (London: Routledge and Kegan Paul, 1973), p. 332.
40. Ibid., p. 333.
41. Ibid., p. 333.

42. Henry Sidgwick, *The Methods of Ethics*, Seventh Edition 1907 (London: Macmillan, 1963), p. 436.
43. *Conservatism*, p. 102.
44. Ibid., p. 104.
45. Ibid., p. 104.
46. Ibid., p. 106.
47. Terry L. Anderson and Donald R. Deal, *Free Market Environmentalism* (Boulder: Westview Press, 1991), p. 164.
48. *Conservatism*, p. 42.
49. Ibid., p. 108.
50. J. J. Thomson, 'A Defence of Abortion', *Philosophy and Public Affairs*, vol. 1, no. 2, 1971, pp. 47–66.
51. J. S. Mill, 'Utilitarianism', in John Stuart Mill, *On Liberty and Other Essays* (Oxford: Oxford University Press, 1991), p. 189.
52. See, for example, Benedict Spinoza, *A Theologico-Political Treatise*.
53. Friedrich Hayek, *The Constitution of Liberty* (London: Routledge and Kegan Paul, 1960), p. 22.
54. Ibid., p. 26.
55. Ibid., p. 26.
56. *Conservatism*, p. 120.
57. Ibid., p. 120.
58. John Gray, *Liberalism* (Milton Keynes: Open University Press, 1986), p. 74.
59. For example, Joan Kennedy-Taylor, *Reclaiming the Mainstream: Individualist Feminism Rediscovered* (New York: Prometheus Books, 1992).
60. Susan Moller Okin, *Women in Western Political Thought* (Princeton, New Jersey: Princeton University Press, 1979), pp. 3–4.
61. Ibid., p. 293.
62. Caroline New and Miriam David, *For the Children's Sake* (Harmondsworth: Penguin, 1985), pp. 41–3.
63. See, for example, *Women and Men in Britain 1991* (London: Equal Opportunities Commission, 1991).
64. George Gilder, 'The Myth of the Role Revolution', in N. Davidson (ed.), *Gender Sanity: The Case Against Feminism* (Lanham: University Press of America, 1989), pp. 231–3.
65. For a review of the evidence, see Anne Moir and David Jessel, *Brain Sex* (London: Michael Joseph, 1989), especially ch. 11.
66. For a good summary of this evidence, see, for example, Ellen Frankel Paul, *Equity and Gender: The Comparable Worth Debate* (New Brunswick: Transaction Publishers, 1989), ch. 2.
67. Quoted in Paul, ibid., p. 44.

4   COMMUNITARIANISM

1. See, for example, John Smith, 'Reclaiming the Ground', R. H. Tawney Memorial Lecture, delivered 20 March 1993.
2. The most prominent representatives of this body of critics of liberalism are Alasdair MacIntyre, Michael Sandel, Charles Taylor, Michael Walzer. For a good introductory exposition of their thought, see Stephen Mulhall and

Adam Swift, *Liberals and Communitarians* (Oxford: Blackwell, 1992) and Shlomo Avineri and Avner de-Shalit (eds), *Communitarianism and Individualism* (Oxford: Oxford University Press, 1992).
3. See Michael J. Sandel, 'Morality and the Liberal Ideal', *The New Republic*, 7 May 1984, pp. 15–17, and 'Democrats and Community', *The New Republic*, 22 February 1988, pp. 20–3.
4. Alasdair MacIntyre, *After Virtue: A Study in Moral Theory*, Second Edition (London: Duckworth, 1985).
5. As well as the references given in note 3, see Michael Sandel, *Liberalism and the Limits of Justice* (Cambridge: Cambridge University Press, 1982).
6. *After Virtue*, p. 172.
7. Ibid., p. 236.
8. Ibid., p. 156.
9. Ibid., p. 156.
10. Ibid., p. 172.
11. Markate Daly (ed.), *Communitarianism: A New Public Ethics* (Belmont, California: Wadsworth, 1994), p. xv.
12. *After Virtue*, p. 156.
13. Ibid., p. 172.
14. Michael Sandel, 'Morality and the Liberal Ideal', *The New Republic*, 7 May 1984, pp. 15–17, p. 17.
15. Michael, J. Sandel, 'Democrats and Community', *The New Republic*, 22 February 1988, pp. 22–3.
16. On this, see A. E. Taylor, *Aristotle* (New York: Dover, 1955), pp. 99–100.
17. Charles Murray, *In Pursuit of Happiness and Good Government* (New York: Simon and Schuster, 1988). See especially ch. 12.
18. Friedrich Hayek, 'Individualism; True and False', in F. Hayek, *Individualism and Economic Order* (Chicago: University of Chicago Press, 1948), p. 6.
19. Ibid., pp. 22–3.
20. *After Virtue*, p. 187.
21. Ibid., pp. 190–1.
22. Ibid., p. 191.
23. Ibid., p. 190.
24. Ibid., p. 187.
25. Ibid., pp. 187–8.
26. Ibid., p. 219.
27. Ibid., p. 222.
28. Ibid., p. 222.
29. Ibid., p. 191.
30. Ibid., p. 191.
31. Ibid., p. 219.
32. Ibid., p. 223.
33. Ibid., p. 223.
34. Ibid., p. 223.
35. Ibid., p. 223.
36. Ibid., p. 195.
37. Ibid., p. 172.
38. See ibid., p. 254.
39. Ibid., p. 227.

40. Ibid., pp. 227–8.
41. Ibid., p. 227.
42. Ibid., p. 222.
43. Ibid., p. 195. Note that I have changed MacIntyre's text here and substituted 'political' for 'parental', since I believe the context of the remark makes clear that this is what he intended to write and that what was printed is a misprint.
44. Ibid., p. 195.
45. Ibid., p. ix.
46. Ibid., p. x.
47. Ibid., p. 259.
48. This account of Aristotle's conception of the human *telos* has been heavily influenced by Richard Kraut, *Aristotle on the Human Good* (Princeton, New Jersey: Princeton University Press, 1989).
49. *After Virtue*, p. 59.
50. Ibid., p. 8.
51. Ibid., p. 231.
52. Ibid., p. 62.
53. Ibid., pp. 63–4.

5 CONSERVATISM

1. Michael Oakeshott, 'On Being Conservative', in Michael Oakeshott, *Rationalism in Politics and Other Essays* (Indianapolis: Liberty Press, 1991), p. 408.
2. See Michael Oakeshott, *Rationalism in Politics and Other Essays* (Indianapolis: Liberty Press, 1991).
3. See David Willetts, *Modern Conservatism* (Harmondsworth: Penguin, 1992).
4. See Roger Scruton, 'In Defence of the Nation', in Roger Scruton, *The Philosopher on Dover Beach* (New York: St. Martin's Press, 1990), 'What is Conservatism?', in *Conservative Texts*, R. Scruton (London: Macmillan; New York: St. Martin's Press, 1991); and 'Totalitarianism, Civil Society and the Nation', *Salisbury Review*, March 1992, pp. 10–14.
5. See John Gray, *Liberalisms* (London: Routledge, 1989); *The Moral Foundations of Market Institutions* (London: IEA Health and Welfare Unit, 1992); *Post-Liberalism* (London and New York: Routledge, 1993).
6. R. Scruton, 'In Defence of the Nation', p. 327.
7. Ibid., p. 319.
8. R. Scruton, 'Hegel as a Conservative Thinker', in R. Scruton, *The Philosopher on Dover Beach* (New York: St. Martin's Press, 1990), p. 51.
9. G. W. F. Hegel, *Philosophy of Right*, ed. T. M. Knox (Oxford: Oxford University Press, 1967), sec. 258, p. 156.
10. R. Scruton, 'Hegel as a Conservative Thinker', pp. 51–2.
11. Charles Taylor, *Hegel* (Cambridge: Cambridge University Press, 1975), p. 387.
12. S. Avineri, *Hegel's Theory of the Modern State* (Cambridge: Cambridge University Press, 1972), p. 119.
13. Ibid., pp. 119–20.
14. F. Hegel, *Philosophy of Right*, Preface, pp. 6–7.

15. Joseph Raz, *The Morality of Freedom* (Oxford: Clarendon Press, 1986).
16. J. Gray, *Moral Foundations of Market Institutions*, p. 22.
17. Isaiah Berlin, *Vico and Herder* (London: Hogarth Press, 1976), pp. 206–7.
18. J. Gray, *Post-Liberalism*, pp. 297–8.
19. Joseph Raz, *The Morality of Freedom* (Oxford: Clarendon Press, 1986), pp. 391–4.
20. J. Gray, *The Moral Foundations of Market Institutions*, p. 26.
21. Ibid., pp. 22–3.
22. J. Gray, *Post-Liberalism*, p. 307.
23. J. Gray, *Moral Foundations of Market Institutions*, p. 63.
24. Ibid., p. 66.
25. Ibid., p. 80.
26. I owe inspiration for both objections to Gray's arguments against classical liberalism to Chandran Kukathas. See his comments on Gray's argument in J. Gray, *Moral Foundations of Market Institutions*.
27. J. Gray, *Post-Liberalism*, p. 246.
28. Ibid., p. 299.
29. Ibid., p. 305.
30. Ibid., p. 313.
31. Ibid., p. 316.
32. Ibid., p. 316.
33. J. Gray, *Liberalisms*, p. 260.
34. Nathaniel Branden, 'Alienation', pp. 279–80 in Ayn Rand, *Capitalism: The Unknown Ideal* (New York: Signet Books, 1967).
35. Michel Albert, *Capitalism Against Capitalism* (London: Whurr Publishers, 1993), pp. 170–2.

6 CONCLUSION

1. See Charles Murray, *In Pursuit of Happiness and Good Government* (New York: Simon and Schuster, 1988), pp. 273–9. See, also, Marvin Olasky, *The Tragedy of American Compassion* (Washington, DC: Regnery Gateway, 1992).
2. For details of the relevant body of research, see Arthur Seldon, *Capitalism* (Oxford: Basil Blackwell, 1990), ch. 11.
3. See Charles Murray, *Losing Ground: American Social Policy 1950–1980* (New York: Basic Books, 1984); Norman Dennis and George Erdos, *Families without Fatherhood* (London: IEA Health and Welfare Unit, 1992); and Norman Dennis, *Rising Crime and the Dismembered Family* (London: IEA Health and Welfare Unit, 1993). See also Charles Murray, *The Emerging British Underclass* (London: IEA Health and Welfare Unit, 1990).
4. See the works of Charles Murray and Norman Dennis mentioned in note 3.

Bibliography

Albert, M., *Capitalism Against Capitalism* (London: Whurr Publishers, 1993).

Anderson, T. L. and Deal, D. R., *Free Market Environmentalism* (Boulder: Westview Press, 1991).

Aristotle, 'Politics', in *Basic Works of Aristotle*, ed. R. McKeon (New York: Random House, 1941).

Avineri, S. and de-Shalit, A. (eds), *Communitarianism and Individualism* (Oxford: Oxford University Press, 1992).

Berlin, I., *Vico and Herder* (London: Hogarth Press, 1976).

Branden, N., 'Alienation' in Ayn Rand, *Capitalism: The Unknown Ideal* (New York: Signet Books, 1967).

Brentano, F., *The Foundation and Construction of Ethics* (London: Routledge and Kegan Paul, 1973).

Dalberg-Acton, J. E. E., 'The History of Freedom in Christianity', in Lord Acton, *Essays in the History of Liberty*, ed. J. R. Fears (Indianapolis: Liberty Press, 1986).

Daly, M. (ed.), *Communitarianism: A New Public Ethics* (Belmont, California: Wadsworth, 1994).

Dennis, N. and Erdos, G., *Families without Fatherhood* (London: IEA Health and Welfare Unit, 1992).

Dennis, N., *Rising Crime and the Dismembered Family* (London: IEA Health and Welfare Unit, 1993).

Dworkin, R., 'Liberalism' in S. Hampshire (ed.), *Public and Private Morality* (Cambridge: Cambridge University Press, 1978).

Dworkin, R., 'What is Equality?' in two parts: Part l, Equality of Welfare, *Philosophy and Public Affairs* (Summer 1981); Part ll, Equality of Resources, *Philosophy and Public Affairs* (Fall 1981).

Dworkin, R., 'Why Liberals Should Believe in Equality', *New York Review of Books* (3 February 1983), pp. 32–4.

Dworkin, R., 'In Defence of Equality', in *Social Philosophy and Policy*, vol. 1, no. 1 (Autumn 1983), pp. 24–40.

Equal Opportunities Commission, *Women and Men in Britain 1991* (London: Equal Opportunities Commission, 1991).

Ferguson, A., *An Essay on the History of Civil Society*, ed. D. Forbes (Edinburgh: Edinburgh University Press, 1966).

Gauthier, D., 'Justice and Natural Endowment: Toward a Critique of Rawls' Ideological Framework', *Social Theory and Practice*, vol. 3, 1974, pp. 3–26.

Gauthier, D., *Morals by Agreement* (Oxford: Clarendon Press, 1986).

Gilder, G., 'The Myth of the Role Revolution' in N. Davidson (ed.), *Gender Sanity: The Case Against Feminism* (Lanham: University Press of America, 1989).

Gray, J., *Liberalism* (Milton Keynes: Open University Press, 1986).

Gray, J., *Liberalisms* (London: Routledge, 1989).

Gray, J., *The Moral Foundations of Market Institutions* (London: IEA Health and Welfare Unit, 1992).

Gray, J., *Post-Liberalism* (London and New York: Routledge, 1993).

Hayek, F., *The Constitution of Liberty* (London: Routledge and Kegan Paul, 1960).
Hayek, F., *Individualism and Economic Order* (Chicago: University of Chicago Press, 1948).
Hegel, G. W. F., *Philosophy of Right*, ed. T. M. Knox (Oxford: Oxford University Press, 1967).
Hobbes, T., *Leviathan*, ed. C. B. Macpherson (Harmondsworth: Penguin, 1968).
Honderich, T., *Conservatism* (London: Hamish Hamilton, 1990).
Kennedy-Taylor, J., *Reclaiming the Mainstream: Individualist Feminism Reconsidered* (New York: Prometheus Books, 1992).
Kraut, R., *Aristotle on the Human Good* (Princeton, New Jersey: Princeton University Press, 1989).
Locke, J., *Two Treatises of Government*, ed. P. Laslett (Cambridge University Press, 1960).
MacIntyre, A., *After Virtue: A Study in Moral Theory*, Second Edition (London: Duckworth, 1985).
Moir, A. and Jessel, D., *Brain Sex* (London: Michael Joseph, 1989).
Mill, J. S., 'Utilitarianism', in *On Liberty and Other Essays* (Oxford: Oxford University Press, 1991).
von Mises, L., *Liberalism* (San Francisco: Cobden Press, 1985).
Mulhall, S. and Swift, A., *Liberals and Communitarians* (Oxford: Blackwell, 1992).
Murray, C., *The Emerging British Underclass* (London: IEA Health and Welfare Unit, 1990).
Murray, C., *In Pursuit of Happiness and Good Government* (New York: Simon and Schuster, 1988).
Murray, C., *Losing Ground: American Social Policy 1950–1980* (New York: Basic Books, 1984).
Nagel, T., *Equality and Partiality* (New York: Oxford University Press, 1991).
New, C. and David, M., *For the Children's Sake* (Harmondsworth: Penguin, 1985).
Nielsen, K., *Equality and Liberty: A Defence of Radical Egalitarianism* (Totowa, New Jersey: Rowman and Allanheld Publishers, 1985).
Nozick, R., *Anarchy, State and Utopia* (New York: Basic Books, 1974).
Oakeshott, M., 'On Being Conservative', in Michael Oakeshott, *Rationalism in Politics and Other Essays* (Indianapolis: Liberty Press, 1991).
Olasky, M., *The Tragedy of American Compassion* (Washington, DC: Regnery Gateway, 1992).
Okin, S. M., *Women in Western Political Thought* (Princeton, New Jersey: Princeton University Press, 1979).
Paul, E. F., *Equity and Gender: The Comparable Worth Debate* (New Brunswick: Transaction Publishers, 1989).
Plato, *Republic*, trans. D. Lee, Second Edition (Harmondsworth: Penguin 1974).
Rawls, J., *A Theory of Justice* (Oxford: Clarendon Press, 1972).
Rawls, J., 'Justice as Fairness: Political not Metaphysical', *Philosophy and Public Affairs*, 1985, vol. 14, pp. 223–51.
Rawls, J., *Political Liberalism* (New York: Columbia University Press, 1993).
Raz, J., *The Morality of Freedom* (Oxford: Clarendon Press, 1986).
Lord Robbins, *Theory of Economic Policy in English Classical Political Economy*, Second Edition (London: Macmillan, 1978).
Sandel, M. J., 'Democrats and Community', *The New Republic*, 22 February 1988.

Sandel, M. J., *Liberalism and the Limits of Justice* (Cambridge: Cambridge University Press, 1982).

Sandel, M. J., 'Morality and the Liberal Ideal', *The New Republic*, 7 May 1984, pp. 15–17.

Scruton, R., 'Hegel as a Conservative Thinker', in Roger Scruton, *The Philosopher on Dover Beach* (New York: St. Martin's Press, 1990).

Scruton, R., 'In Defence of the Nation', in Roger Scruton, *The Philosopher on Dover Beach* (New York: St. Martin's Press, 1990).

Scruton, R., 'Totalitarianism, Civil Society and the Nation', *Salisbury Review*, March 1992, pp. 10–14.

Scruton, R., 'What is Conservatism? in (ed.) R. Scruton, *Conservative Texts* (London: Macmillan; St. Martin's Press, 1991).

Seldon, A., *Capitalism* (Oxford: Basil Blackwell, 1990).

Sidgwick, H., *The Elements of Politics* (London: Macmillan, 1891).

Sidgwick, H., *The Methods of Ethics*, Seventh Edition 1907 (London: Macmillan, 1963).

Smith, A., *The Theory of Moral Sentiments* (Indianapolis: Liberty Classics, 1976).

Smith, A., *The Wealth of Nations*, vol. 2., eds R. H. Campbell and A. S. Skinner (Shadeland, Indianapolis: Liberty Press, 1979).

Smith, J., 'Reclaiming the Ground', R. H. Tawney Lecture, delivered 20 March 1993.

Spinoza, Benedict, 'A Theologico-Political Treatise' in *The Chief Works of Benedict Spinoza*, trans. R. H. M. Elwes (New York: Dover, 1951).

Taylor, A. E., *Aristotle* (New York: Dover, 1955).

Taylor, C., *Hegel* (Cambridge: Cambridge University Press, 1975).

Thomson, J. J., 'A Defence of Abortion', *Philosophy and Public Affairs*, vol. 1, no. 2, 1971, pp. 47–66.

Willets, D., *Modern Conservatism* (Harmondsworth: Penguin, 1992).